ETHICS

AN EARLY AMERICAN HANDBOOK

A Reprint of an 1890 Original

Aledo, Texas

Ethics: An Early American Handbook

For additional copies of this book, or for information on other books and reprints, contact:
WallBuilders
426 Circle Dr.
P.O. Box 397
Aledo, TX 76008
(817) 441-6044
For orders and catalog, call (800) 873-2845
www.wallbuilders.com

Cover Design
Jeremiah Pent
Lincoln-Jackson
3843 Winslow Dr.
Ft. Worth, TX 76109
(817) 922-8450
www.lincolnjackson.com

Cover Portrait
Currier & Ives
The Inauguration of Washington: As First President of the United States
Image 57.100.27
Depicted Date: April 30, 1789; Engraving Date: 1876
Museum of the City of New York
The Harry T. Peters Collection

ISBN 0-925279-72-2
Printed in the United States of America

A

PRIMER OF ETHICS.

EDITED BY

BENJAMIN B. COMEGYS,

Author of "Talks with Boys and Girls," "Beginning Life," "How to Get On," "Old Stories with New Lessons," "Addresses to the Pupils of Girard College," Etc.

——○○✥○○——

GINN & COMPANY

BOSTON · NEW YORK · CHICAGO · LONDON

"The thing that can be done is to introduce into every public school a simple text-book of Ethics, and drill it into every child from the youngest to the oldest. The little book should present the principles of the moral conduct in the clearest and simplest manner; that is, the fundamental ideas of right and wrong, the proper relations in the family, of parent and child, of the young to the old, of inferior to superior, of the employer to the employed, the citizen and the state — the duties in all their relations, as well as the rights. We may then get back a little reverence in place of the growing bumptiousness and smartness. The scholar will then be furnished with the means of seeing the difference of right and wrong in business, in politics, in social life; and added to this, the teacher will be more anxious to develop the mind as a reasoning machine than to stuff it with facts for an examination."

CHARLES DUDLEY WARNER.

The Athenæum Press

GINN & COMPANY · PRO-
PRIETORS · BOSTON · U.S.A.

PREFACE.

———•◦•———

JACOB ABBOTT was, in his day, the most voluminous, the most popular, the most useful writer for the young.

One of his books, "The Rollo Code of Morals," has been out of print for many years. By permission of his family and his publishers, I have prepared a new edition of this book for the use of young people at school and at home.

My work has been largely that of abbreviation and modern adaptation; but some chapters have been omitted and some new ones added.

For some thoughts in the chapter on "Duties to Dumb Creatures," I am indebted to my friend, Professor Fullerton, of the University of Pennsylvania.

I am very grateful to Dr. Mackenzie, Head Master of the Lawrenceville School, New Jersey, and to Dr. Fetterolf, President of Girard College, who have read the book in manuscript, for many most valuable hints.

The book is only a Primer; but its principles are of much wider application.

B. B. COMEGYS.

PHILADELPHIA, 4205 Walnut Street.

MR. ABBOTT'S PREFACE.

THERE are few teachers who do not feel the need of some additional means and facilities to aid them in the cultivation of the moral sentiments of their pupils ; but to provide these facilities is a very difficult and delicate task. It is true that nothing is easier than to write lectures inculcating moral truth ; and, at the same time, scarcely anything is more difficult than to convey such instruction so as to secure admission for it to the minds and hearts of children, and a permanent influence there. This little work, however, is an attempt to accomplish this object. It consists of a series of lessons, designed to explain and illustrate to young children their most simple and obvious duties, and those traits of moral character which it is most desirable should be early formed.

The teacher will observe that each lesson consists of three distinct portions : —

1. A general statement of the principle or duty about to be explained and enforced. It stands at the head of the lesson, and is intended to be committed to memory by the class. It may be recited by the whole of the

class in rotation, or by any part of it, either before the
reading, or immediately before the questions upon the
reading, which are given at the close of the lesson ; or
the committing of it to memory may be dispensed with
entirely — according to the discretion of the teacher.

2. There follows an explanation, illustration, and
enforcement of the principle. This reading should be
accompanied with suitable explanations and remarks
by the teacher. The writer has endeavored to present
the subjects discussed in such points of view as to
awaken the attention and excite the interest of children ; but, in treating the subjects, he has not confined himself to the language of children, as one great
object of such an exercise is to advance the pupils'
knowledge of language, and add to their vocabulary of
English words. It will be desirable, therefore, that the
teacher should frequently question the readers about
the meaning of words, and take other measures to secure
the full understanding of the lesson by the class ; and it
will be especially beneficial if the various topics discussed
lead to additional remarks and explanations by the
teacher, and to conversations with the members of the
class, in order that their minds may be made thoroughly
familiar with the principles which the book inculcates.

3. To each lesson is added a series of questions.
Some of these arise directly from the lessons ; others
relate to the subject generally, and the answer is to be
furnished by the pupil himself from his own reflections.

These questions, or a part of them, with such others as the teacher may add, can be put to the class, in succession, at the close of each exercise. The pupil should be encouraged to use his own language in expressing his replies; and, in fact, it will be observed, as has been before intimated, that there are questions for which no direct answers can be found in the lessons, and which the pupil must consequently answer from his own reflections, and in his own language. They are intended to lead him to reflect upon what he has read, and, by thus exercising his thinking and reasoning powers, to strengthen his judgment and cultivate his moral sense.

CONTENTS.

———◦◇◦———

A PRIMER OF ETHICS.

———∘○⟨⊚⟩○∘———

TRUTH.

Truth is sincerity; and in all we say and do, we must be sincere. We must not make false impressions, directly or indirectly.

THERE are many ways by which we may mislead and deceive others by what we say; and these ways differ very much from each other in criminality. Some of the principal of them are these :—

1. Saying a thing when we know it is not true.
2. Saying a thing when we do not know whether it is true or not.
3. Prevaricating.
4. Misrepresenting.
5. Exaggerating.

All these are different forms of untruth; let us consider them in order :—

1. Saying a thing when we know it is not true. This is absolute falsehood; and whoever is habitually guilty of it after he is old enough to understand the nature of the sin, is depraved. Young people are perhaps most frequently led into this sin at first by having committed some other fault, and then telling a lie to conceal it. Sometimes there are circumstances which seem to draw

one into the falsehood without any previous intention to say what is not true. A boy was led to tell a false-hood in this way, very much as many others have been.

There was a deep pond behind his father's garden. Early in the winter it froze over. One morning he took the axe from the shed, and cut a hole in the ice to fish. After he had cut the hole, the axe slipped from his hands, fell through the hole, and went to the bottom. The boy ought to have gone at once and told his father; but he was afraid to do this, and so he said nothing about it.

Shortly after this, his father wanted the axe, and told his son to see if he could find it. If his father had asked him directly if he knew where it was, probably he would have told him the truth; but, as he asked him to look for it, the boy said nothing, but went and looked in the shed, and in the barn, and in the shop, and then came back, and said the axe was nowhere to be found. This was dishonest, but it was not strictly false. He had said, thus far, nothing which was not true; but he was gradually getting himself entangled in a difficulty which, it might easily be seen, would probably lead him to a direct falsehood.

His father, thinking it very strange that the axe should disappear, went with his son to look for it, and, on the way, he abruptly asked him whether he could not recollect having had it lately; and the boy hastily answered, "No." He had only an instant to reflect; and in that instant the thought flashed through his mind that he could not now confess that he had lost the axe, without exposing the deception he had practised in pretending to look for it, and also the thought that it was some time before this that he had lost the axe; and his father's question was, whether he had seen it lately. This enabled him to quiet his conscience a little, and to flatter himself that he was not telling an absolute lie. The next moment, his father asked him whether he had seen it anywhere since they were splitting the log in the shed; and he answered, "No, sir." His father then went away; and the son sat down on a log before the wood-pile, and covered his face with his hands, over-whelmed with the bitter reflection that he had been gradually led on to tell his father an absolute and un-qualified lie. His peace of mind was destroyed. All that afternoon and evening he was afraid to meet his father, for fear he would say something about the axe. The sight of the shed, of the wood-pile, of the ice, and even of the wood burning in the fire-place, seemed to recall to his mind the thoughts of his sin; and he was afraid all the time, that his father would go down to the pond, and see the hole cut in the ice, and so would dis-cover his guilt. At first, he thought that the hole would soon freeze over again; but then he reflected that it would leave a sort of scar upon the spot, which would, perhaps, remain all winter to reproach and betray him. At night he could not sleep; and at last he was so mis-erable that he got up and went to his father's chamber, and confessed that he had lost the axe through the ice, and had told falsehoods about it; and he said that he was so wretched in consequence, that he did not know what to do.

It is very often in a way somewhat like this that young people are led to tell their first wilful falsehoods. Then, unless they go and confess them honestly, as this boy did, they bear the reproaches of conscience for a time, until they gradually forget the offence; and then, on the next occasion, they commit the sin a little more deliberately, and with less compunction. They go on very fast in the downward course, when they have thus begun. They say what is false more and more frequently and boldly, until, at length, they are ready at any time to tell a lie to conceal their faults, or to gain their wishes. Their characters always become known; neither their parents nor their teachers can believe them; and even their acquaintances know that there is no dependence to be placed upon anything they say.

2. The second form of untruthfulness mentioned is:— making a statement when we do not know whether it is true or not. A woman went away one afternoon, and left the house in charge of her daughter, directing her to stay in the house, and attend to any one who might come. After her mother had gone, the daughter went to play in the garden, until just before the time for her mother to return; and then, when her mother came home, and asked her if there had been anybody there, she said "No."

Now, this was not a direct and absolute falsehood; but there was an indirect falsehood implied in it; because, when she said that nobody had called at the house, she wished her mother to understand that she had been faithful at her post, and knew that what she said was true. Her mother did understand her so, and was deceived; so there was falsehood involved in her answer, though it was not directly expressed. A farmer asked his boy if the cows were all in the barn-yard, and the boy said, "Yes," when he did not know whether they were there or not, but only supposed they were there, and did not wish to take the trouble to go and see. A man had a horse to sell, and said that he was only seven years old, when he did not know how old he was. Now, both these persons were guilty of indirect falsehood. The falsehood was not absolute and express, as it would have been if the boy had known that the cows were not all in the yard, and if the man had known that his horse was more than seven years old. They presumed, and hoped, that what they said was true; but they did not know that it was true; and, by asserting it as if they did know, and by intending to lead others to suppose that they knew, they were guilty of indirect falsehood. There is very much of this kind of falsehood in the world. Many persons, who would on no account say what they know to be false, often say what they have no sufficient reason for believing to be true.

3. Prevaricating. This means saying something which is not in itself strictly and absolutely false, but which is intended to convey a false meaning; as, when a boy said that he had not a single nut in his pocket, while in fact, he had many. When the nuts were found there, he attempted to justify himself by saying he had not a single nut — he had several. A man had a house to sell, and the purchaser asked him whether it had a good well of water, and he answered that the water was excellent, and it afterwards appeared that, though the water was excellent while it lasted, yet that the well was dry for two months in the summer. This man was guilty of prevarication. It is a kind of falsehood which is very common. Even if not so wicked as an absolute lie, it is very wrong. We ought never to say what will make a false impression.

4. Misrepresentation.   We misrepresent when we tell
a part of the truth and conceal the rest ; or when we
distort or color it, in the interest of our own feelings.
When two boys have any disagreement or contention,
and attempt to give an account of the circumstances to
their mother or teacher, they almost always misrepresent
the case.   Each conceals or passes over very slightly
what he himself did which was wrong, and states very
emphatically and strongly what the other did which was
wrong.   A boy is knocking a ball, and the bat accidentally hits another boy, and *he* complains that the first
boy struck him with a great stick ; this is misrepresentation.   It gives a wrong idea.   This is a fault to which
all persons are exposed.   Yet it is a kind of falsehood.
We are led into it by our feelings, by anger, by irritation, by our desire to gain our point, whatever that may
be, and by other strong emotions.   But we ought to
guard against it with the greatest care, and watch ourselves, especially when our feelings are strongly interested in any case, lest we turn truth into falsehood, by
intentional or unintentional misrepresentation.

5. Exaggeration.   This is lying by representing anything greater than it really is ; as when a boy says that
he has been trying very hard indeed, for a long time, to
do a certain example on his slate, when he had not, in
fact, been very diligent, and had only been employed
upon the work a short time.   Young people exaggerate
their sickness sometimes, when they are only a little
unwell, but want to be excused from going to school,
or from doing some work.   They exaggerate the difficulties in doing anything they do not want to do ; and,
in describing what they have seen or done, they often

make it much greater or more wonderful than it really was. Travellers often exaggerate the dangers they have passed through, or the marvellousness of the sights which they have seen. There are very few persons, whether old or young, whose accounts of what they see and hear can be fully depended upon, as strictly accurate and just. Their feelings, their interests, and even the excitement of conversation or of argument, are often sufficient to lead them to overstate facts, so that their statements cannot be depended upon. Yet, by all these exaggerations, truth is sacrificed.

QUESTIONS.

There are several ways mentioned at the beginning of the lesson, by which we may deceive and mislead others ; name any of them that you can recollect. *Which is said to be the worst of them ?*

How is it that boys are generally led to begin to speak falsehood? Describe the case of the boy who lost the axe.

When he said that he could not find the axe, did he tell an absolute lie? Was he dishonest?

What ought he to have done when he first lost the axe?

What is the second offence against truth, which is mentioned in the lesson?

Tell the story of the girl left in charge of a house.

Did she know that what she stated was not true?

Was she to blame for saying nobody had been there? Was she as much to blame as she would have been if she had known that somebody had been there, and yet had said what she did?

Do you remember any other cases of this kind of falsehood?

What is prevaricating?

How is this seen in the case of the man who had a house to sell? What is misrepresentation?

Which do you think is most common, prevarication or misrepresentation?

Is prevarication always intentional?

Is misrepresentation always intentional?

Which should you consider generally the more wicked, to prevaricate or to misrepresent?

In what cases are children under very strong temptation to misrepresent?

Did you ever know any children who would not misrepresent in such cases?

What is exaggeration? Can you give an example of it?

Do you think these principles are too strict?

Should you like to have all your playmates and companions live up to them?

Can lies be told without speaking words?

How can any one act a lie?

How early in life can a child tell lies?

May persons who are known to be saying extravagant things for fun do so without lying?

How? Nobody is deceived.

How can any one think a lie?

Is this as bad as a spoken lie?

Are people often tempted to tell lies?

Can a liar have the respect of good people?

What are lying lips said to be?

OBEDIENCE.

Obedience is doing what is commanded, or not doing what is forbidden, because it is commanded or forbidden by one who has authority. Obedience should be prompt, faithful and cheerful.

In the various circumstances in which we are placed in life we are all under obligation to obey. The soldier must obey his officer, the sailor must obey his com mander, the apprentice must obey his master, and every citizen must obey the laws of the land. Children and youth are under special obligations to obey their parents, their teachers and their guardians. In all these, and in many other cases, persons are bound to obey.

Now, obedience is doing what is commanded, because it is commanded, and not because we think it is best to do it.

It is important to understand this, because it often happens that when young people receive a command from their parents or teachers, instead of obeying it, they stop to ask for the reason of it, — as if it were necessary that they should understand the reason before they obey. This is wrong. When we are commanded to do anything by a person who has authority, we ought to do it because it is commanded, and not because we see a reason for it. It is very proper for young people to wish to know the reasons for their parents' commands ; but they must never delay their obedience to

9

inquire. They should obey first, and ask the reason afterwards.

A child may know what the reason of the command is, and yet not be satisfied with it : and think, on that account he may refuse to obey. His father tells him not to go upon a certain piece of ice, because he thinks it is not strong enough to bear him ; and the boy thinks it is strong enough : but he ought to obey, not because he sees the command is reasonable, but because it is a command. So the sailor must take in sail at once, when the captain orders him to do it, even if he thinks it ought not to be taken in ; and the apprentice, or the boy, or man, ought to do the work as the master or employer directs, even if he thinks he knows a better way.

And more than this : a case may happen in which a boy may know that his father or mother was mistaken, and that the command was an unnecessary one ; still it ought to be obeyed. A farmer once was sending his boy some miles to a grist-mill, and he told him to go round by the bridge to get across the stream, as the fording-place was not safe. Now, the boy knew that it was safe ; he had crossed the ford many times, and he knew that his father was mistaken. His father was old, and feeble, and timid, and his son was sure that he was needlessly afraid. Still he obeyed him. He might have taken the short road through the ford, instead of going round by the bridge, and his father would probably never have known of his disobedience. But he would not disobey. He knew that the reason why he must obey his father, was not because it was certain that his father would always be right, but because he was his father, and that he had the right to command his son. This is the very nature of obedience, and young people should understand that it is obedience which they owe to their parents. When, therefore, a boy's father or mother directs him to do anything, he must remember that it is a command, not advice; and therefore it is not necessary that he should know or be satisfied with the reasons, or refuse to obey because he is not told them.

Obedience ought to be prompt; that is, the command must be obeyed as soon as it is given, or at the time directed. Sometimes children delay, ask the reason for the command, or make objections; sometimes they are doing something else which they do not wish to leave; and sometimes, when the duty is not very pleasant, they move so slowly and reluctantly in doing it, as to consume more time than is necessary to accomplish the object.

Prompt obedience is worth much more than that which is reluctant and slow. He who obeys tardily does not more than half obey. He who moves slowly when he is told to do something; who spends much time in making preparations to do it; who stops to ask questions, or to make objections, or to propose some other way; who loiters when sent with a message, and who puts off as long as he can every duty, — such a boy would be of very little service to his employer.

Then, too, prompt obedience is much the more pleasant. If a disagreeable duty is to be performed, the easiest way to get through it is to do it at once. Two boys have paths to make every morning after a snow-storm. One, as soon as he is dressed, is out at his work, facing the cool morning air as a General would

face an enemy.   The other peeps out to see if it is cold;
then comes back and stands for a long time about the
fire, putting on his mittens and warming his feet, and
dreading his work.   At last he is just ready to begin
when the first boy is finishing.   Which, now, gets
through his work more easily and pleasantly ? The way
to make a disagreeable or painful duty as disagreeable
and painful as possible, is to perform it in a reluctant,
inefficient and dilatory manner.

Obedience ought to be cheerful.   It must necessarily
be that many commands which we have to obey are
disagreeable.   Still they must be obeyed ; and they are
made much more disagreeable to all concerned by being
obeyed in a sullen and ill-natured manner.   The commands which are given to young people are of different
kinds ; but there is good reason for obeying them cheerfully and pleasantly.   Some are given solely upon the
child's own account, to do him some good, as when he is
sent to school ; or to save him from future suffering, as
when he is required to take medicine when he is sick,
or when he is told to put down a penknife with which
he wants to play.   Many of the restraints and privations which are imposed upon children are of this kind.
They are for their own good.   It is true this is not
enough to make them agreeable to bear, but it is enough
to make it the duty of a child to bear them cheerfully
and without murmuring.   Other commands are for the
benefit of the parent, as when there is work to do, or a
message to carry, or a young child to be watched and
taken care of.   These duties often come at a time when
children find it very inconvenient to attend to them ;
but they must be attended to ; and whatever we have to

give up of our own wishes and plans, to help a father or mother, or any other person, ought to be given up cheerfully. Those children who have any sense of gratitude, and who consider how many painful, and wearisome, and long-continued anxieties and labors the parent has suffered for the child, without a word of repining, will not think it right to repine at any inconveniences they can be called upon to submit to in return.

Obedience ought to be faithful. When any work is to be done by boys and girls, they ought to go forward as steadily and industriously when they are not watched as when they are. It is not enough to go through the forms of obedience. If a boy should be set to write or to study for an hour, in a room by himself, he must not only remain there at his post, but he must give his mind diligently to his work. A faithful boy will do so whether he is observed or not. He is impelled by an inward principle of duty, and by a desire for the satisfaction and happiness which fidelity will always secure. And so in school. Faithful boys know from experience that the time passes most pleasantly when they are most industriously employed. They do not think it enough, merely to sit still while the mind is straying far away.

There are many different ways of giving commands. Thus, in a ship at sea, the orders of an officer are sometimes given by his own voice, sometimes in writing, sometimes by a messenger, sometimes by peculiar flags hung out as signals, and sometimes even by a whistle. The boatswain has a peculiar kind of whistle, which he blows in various ways, so as to tell the sailors when they must pull upon a rope, and when they must cease

pulling ; when they must come up on deck and when
they must go down.   The shrill whistle can be heard
more distinctly amidst the roar of the winds and waves
than other sounds.   You know in a street car, orders to
stop or go on are given by pulling a bell.   Many of the
orders given to the engineer of a railway train are given
by bells, or by whistles which are sounded through the
air-brakes, or by electric wires.   So in the army, men
are directed by the cavalry bugle and tap of drum.

Now, it makes no difference in which of these ways
an order is given.   The sailors, engineers and soldiers
are bound to obey in one case as much as in another.
And so with children in a family or pupils in a school ;
they are bound to obey their parents and teachers, in
whatever way the order is communicated.   A boy who
does not come in when the bell rings, disobeys.   The
touch of bell was the order.   If a mother beckons to
a child who is out at play, it is a command to come
in, as certainly as the most decided language could be.
If a direction is sent from a parent, by the youngest
child as a messenger, it is to be obeyed as promptly and
faithfully as if it were delivered by the parent himself.
All that is necessary is, that the wish of the parent
should be made known ; it is certainly immaterial in
what manner this is done.

Young people and children are bound also to obey the
laws of the state or commonwealth.   A boy or girl has
no more right than a man or woman would have, to
disobey laws made for the protection of property or the
security of the rights of others.   The sign "Trespass-
ing forbidden under the penalty of the law," is a command to be observed by children as well as grown people.

A boy who fires a toy pistol or uses a sling-shot within limits forbidden by law, is as truly a bad citizen as a man who commits an act which brings him under punishment of the law.

Such is the kind of obedience which young people ought to render to their parents, to their teachers and to the state; and they ought to render it of their own accord and willingly, without making it necessary to exercise force. But if they will not obey of their own accord, it is most undoubtedly the parent's or teacher's duty to compel them to obey. This is a very painful duty, but it must be performed. Children are not old enough to understand the reasons for all the commands and prohibitions which their parents or teachers think necessary. In some cases where they might understand, there is not time to explain them. Then, even where the reasons can be understood, and are fully explained, young people, as we all know perfectly well, cannot be depended upon to do what they know is best, without being required to do it. They have not sufficient firmness, constancy and self-denial. It is not reasonable to expect it of them. It becomes necessary, by the very nature of their minds, that there should be a power above them, to make up, by its authority, for their want of mental and moral energy and self-control. Parents and teachers must therefore have authority. They cannot depend upon advice or persuasion; they must command. And children must obey. Obedience is absolutely necessary to good government in the family, the school, and the state.

QUESTIONS.

Are men as well as children often under obligation to obey?

What cases can you mention where men have to obey?

What is meant by obeying?

When we have a command to obey, is it necessary that we should understand the reasons for it?

Is it wrong for us to wish to know the reasons for it?

Is it right to postpone obeying the command in order that we may ask the reasons for it?

Is it any excuse for not obeying, that the reasons do not seem satisfactory?

Suppose we know our parents are mistaken, must we obey? Would it be hard to obey good-humoredly in such a case? Would it be duty to obey?

What case is given to illustrate this?

What is meant by prompt obedience?

Describe the case of the two boys.

What is the meaning of prohibition?

Is it possible that the commands and prohibitions of a parent should always be pleasant?

Is it possible that they should be obeyed pleasantly?

Do you recollect anything which is said of faithful obedience?

Must children obey the laws of the state?

How can they disobey them?

Mention some of the different ways by which commands are given at sea.

Do these different ways cause any difference in regard to the duty of obeying?

In what different ways do parents sometimes communicate their orders? Is the obligation to obey of the same nature in all these cases?

Can young people be depended upon always to do what they ought to do, when they know what it is?

Is it necessary, then, that they should be made to obey?

Suppose they will not do it of their own accord, what is the duty of the parent or teacher?

Can there be good government anywhere without obedience?

INDUSTRY.

Industry is constant diligence in any proper employment ; and we are happier when employed than when idle.

INDUSTRY, to be most successful, must be steady, persevering and wisely directed.

1. Industry ought to be steady. When a young boy and a man of maturity and experience go out together to work, we shall see a very marked difference in their manner. They go into the forest, on a winter morning, with a sled drawn by oxen, to get in wood. The boy is running hither and thither, and jumping about the sled ; and when he comes to the woods he begins cutting, with great zeal and earnestness, to see if he cannot get a log cut off sooner than the man. The man moves deliberately. He takes no unnecessary steps ; he makes no violent exertion. The boy is exhausted in an hour, and after that can do very little more ; while the man is able to continue his labor steadily till the sun goes down in the evening.

Industry to be steady must not be violent ; and the most effectual way to accomplish any purpose is, generally, to exert ourselves with moderation, and then we can continue to work longer.

Boys and girls are very often unsteady in what they do. It is not because they mean to do wrong ; it results from the nature of youth, which is, to be ardent, but

easily fatigued. So when sent upon an errand, they will
set off upon the run, and then, when half-way to their
place of destination, they sit down to rest. When work
is given them, they begin with the greatest energy ; but
in a few minutes their breath is spent, their strength is
gone.   Now, industry must be steady.   The work
should be begun with moderation, so that the strength
may endure.   Emergencies of haste or danger require
extraordinary exertions, no doubt ; but for ordinary
duties, it is best always to begin in such a way as to
be able to go on ; and then we must have resolution to
go on steadily to the end.

2. Industry must be persevering. One cause of want
of perseverance among some persons, is their loss of
interest in what they have begun, so they abandon it
for something else. Thus they go on, and waste time
and strength upon unfinished undertakings. There was
a boy who began to build himself a little shop. He got
the boards together, and sawed some of them so as to
make them of the proper length. This consumed all
his leisure time for two days. Then he saw a squirrel
upon a wood-pile, and that put it in his head to make a
trap. He worked upon this trap until he got it all ready
to nail together, when one day a boy brought a boat to
school, rigged very prettily, and then he concluded to
make a boat as soon as possible. Thus he abandoned
one thing after another and in the end accomplished
nothing. He worked many days upon his shop, trap
and boat, but he produced nothing which was of any
value whatever.   We cannot expect, when we begin
large undertakings, that the interest with which we began will continue to the end. As soon as the novelty

is gone, and the exertions begin to tire, then those who are only stimulated by novelty and momentary zeal, find their energies failing, and the undertaking is abandoned. But the persevering press on. Resolution and energy come in to take the place of the excited interest with which they began, and they go on with firmness and steadiness of purpose till their object is accomplished. Labor, without perseverance, is often wasted.

Young people very often show a want of perseverance in the studies which they begin in school. When some new study is spoken of, they are very desirous of undertaking it. They are sure that they will like it. And so they will like the beginning of it, which is all that they can distinctly foresee ; and the interest and pleasure which really belong to the novelty of the undertaking they think will attach permanently to the study itself. They begin with great zeal ; but when the first ardor is over, and they find that the new study, which looked so attractive, requires the same hard work that the old studies did, they are disappointed and discouraged, and their interest is gone. The remedy for this is to understand very fully, and never forget, that all undertakings, pursuits and studies, after the impulse and novelty of the first onset are over, demand patient and persevering application for their successful accomplishment ; and then, when the excitement and interest of novelty fail, we may hope that a spirit of perseverance and energy will take their place.

3. Industry must be well directed. Making a railroad is a well-directed industry. The interest and pleasure of construction are great, and the road is a public convenience. So is the building of a ship or a bridge. Chil-

dren waste time in doing things which they have not the
power to finish, and sometimes upon things which will
do them no good and give them no pleasure if they do
succeed in completing them. A boy undertook to make
a little saw-mill, on a stream. He found an old saw-
plate, which he was going to use for the saw of his mill;
and then with the tools which his father had, he undertook to make the wheels and the frames, and to fit all
the parts together.   But the work was beyond his
power.   After spending much time and labor, he had
to give up the work in despair. His industry was ill
directed.   Another boy has undertaken to keep two
balls in the air, catching one as it comes down, while
the other is going up. He practises every day, sometimes an hour at a time, and perseveres wonderfully.
But his industry is ill directed. The accomplishment
will be good for nothing but to make idle boys wonder,
when he has learned to do it. Two boys are building a
bridge across a stream where they often go to play.
They are laying a solid abutment of stone at the edge
of each bank, constructing them carefully, as they have
seen masons build a wall. They have selected a plank,
which they are going to place across, when the abut-
ments which are to support the ends of the plank are
completed. This is well-directed industry. There is a
reasonable prospect that they can accomplish the work,
and they will have the pleasure of crossing and recross-
ing upon their bridge for months and months after all
the labor of building has been forgotten.

Much of the industry of men, as well as that of boys,
is wasted in ill-directed efforts. Sometimes, for want of
proper care and deliberation in forming the plan, the

whole enterprise fails. Sometimes they attempt to do what is impossible; and sometimes, after a long period of toil and anxiety and heavy expenditure, they accomplish their object; but they find that it entirely disappoints their expectations and hopes when it is obtained. Therefore, in all our undertakings, whether in the play of childhood or in the serious pursuits of life, we ought to consider whether it is worth while to do what we propose, and if so, how it shall be done, before we begin to expend our energies upon it; and thus our industry will be wisely directed. If we are steady and persevering also, the results may be of great value.

QUESTIONS.

What is industry?

What is necessary to make it successful?

What may be the consequence of a too eager beginning of any work?

Is it easy for young persons to be steady in their work?

Is it easy for them to be steady in their studies?

How must we begin our labors if we wish to go on steadily?

What is perseverance?

Give an account of the management of the boy who did not stick to one thing.

Was he industrious?

Was his industry persevering?

How do children often manifest a want of perseverance in school?

What is it generally, in new studies, that really interests them?

Can the interest of novelty be expected to last long?

What is the example of a well-directed industry?

What is an abutment?

Do men as well as children often waste their strength in ill-directed efforts?

What do you think of the boy and his balls?

Have we any time to waste in this way?

HONESTY.

It is wrong to take the property of others without their consent, or to get any advantage from them by deception or concealment, or any false contrivance. He who does this, or attempts to do it, or even desires to do it, is not honest.

PROPERTY is something which one owns and has a right to own; it may be a house, a farm, a ship, a box of tools, money in the bank or in the pocket, a horse, a dog, a penknife, a pencil, a watch, an apple, a book, or anything else.

People own these things because they have received them as presents, or have inherited them from friends who have died, or have bought them with their own money, or have earned them by labor or by good behavior. Everything which you see or touch belongs to you or to somebody else. If it belongs to you, you have the right to do what you please with it, provided you do not abuse it : if it belongs to somebody else, you have no right to it whatever.

Property may be disposed of, or may be got rid of, by giving it away, by trading with it, that is, by giving one thing for another, by selling it for money, by wasting it in bad living, or by actually destroying it.

The grossest form of dishonesty is stealing — taking the property of another without his knowledge and consent — a sin which is and must be severely condemned and punished. Some people are constantly watching for opportunities to steal. They are thieves, and are feared and abhorred by all. When one of them steals something, the whole community is interested in detecting him, and he is hunted by the officers of justice till he is taken, convicted and sent to prison. He is the common enemy of mankind.

Another class of dishonest acts are frauds. Defrauding is cheating. There are many people who will not steal, being afraid of the prison, and yet they will be guilty of dishonesty by defrauding those who deal with them. Though these people may be very secret and careful in their frauds, their characters gradually become known : they are suspected and shunned, and they can never enjoy their ill-gotten gains. Whatever comes by dishonesty brings a sting with it which destroys the pleasure of having it. It is far better to be perfectly honest, for then our consciences will be at rest : we can meet every one without misgiving or fear, and whatever we have, we can enjoy, — feeling that it is entirely our own. Perfect honesty means several things.

1. An honest boy will not take any property which belongs to other persons without their full consent, either expressed or understood. There are many ways in which property is exposed, and must be exposed, and those who are dishonest can take it if they choose. Property is exposed in families, which children may take. Parents are not generally suspicious of their own children, and do not always watch them very closely to prevent their taking without leave what they like. And sometimes children persuade themselves that to take money, or fruit, or anything else, from their parents, is not so

wicked as it would be to take it from other persons. But it certainly is as wicked ; in fact, in one respect it is more so ; for to the guilt of theft is added the guilt of ingratitude and treachery. Is it any the less wicked to steal from a benefactor and friend, than to steal from a stranger ? Our deceitful hearts always lead us to excuse ourselves for our own particular sins ; but conscience cannot be entirely silenced in respect to this. It warns and remonstrates very loudly when the guilty child is going secretly to the forbidden drawer or closet. It destroys his peace of mind, it makes him afraid to meet the eye of his father or mother, and it punishes him with its painful sting long after the pleasure is over, which his dishonesty secured for him.

2. A boy who is honest will not take advantage of another person by stealth or deception. Such a boy once asked a gentleman to let him ride his horse a little way ; and he was told he might ride him to the stream, which was about a half-mile off, and let him drink. The boy rode to the stream, and there he found another and larger boy on another horse, who asked him to ride a little farther down the road, saying that the owner of the horse would never know it. The younger boy would not go. He had an instinctive feeling that it would be wrong. And it would have been wrong. It would have been dishonest. He would have taken something by stealth and deception, without the owner's consent. What was it that he would have taken ? Why, the use of the horse for a longer period than he had obtained leave to use him. The pleasure of a ride as far as the stream he could have honestly ; but if he had tried to extend the pleasure any farther, it would have been pleasure dishonestly gained.

A man hires a horse to go on a journey of twenty miles, and then at the end of that journey goes on ten miles farther, intending to say nothing about it when he returned. He is not honest. He would save a little money, but he would lose his peace of mind. We must not only not steal property itself, but we must not steal the use of property, nor take it in any way without the owner's consent, either expressed or implied; for the owner has as good a right to the use of his property as he has to the property itself; and to deprive him of one by stealth or deception is as truly dishonest as to deprive him of the other. There is a difference in the degree of guilt. It is more dishonest to take a thing altogether than it is to take the use of it without the owner's consent; but both sins are the same in kind.

Some street-cars have drivers, but not conductors. A boy gets on the back platform to ride without paying. He clings to the car until the driver comes back to send him off. The boy steps off until the driver goes back to his horses, and then gets on again. When asked why he does it, he says it is "good fun." But this boy is really trying to steal a ride — and he is beginning to steal.

Sometimes it is right to take what belongs to another without the owner's expressed consent. The consent may be implied or taken for granted. If you are riding along a farm in the country, where there are wild raspberry bushes, it would be right for you to gather as many raspberries as you wish without asking the consent of the owner of the land. The reason is, it is so universally understood that any person may gather wild raspberries, that the owner's consent, though it has not been expressed in words, is implied. You have good reason to know that the owner would have no objection. If you were spending some days on a visit at a friend's house, and your friend had gone out one morning, and had left you alone in the house, and if you wished to write a letter home, and you were to take out a sheet of paper from a drawer and write your letter and send it away, it would not be dishonest. True, you would have taken the property of another person without any expressed consent, but still consent would have been implied. You might know that your friend would be perfectly willing that you should have the paper; and if she were to return while you were writing the letter, you would not feel guilty and afraid, and attempt to hide the paper away as if you had done something wrong.

In these instances the value of the property is very small. But upon the same principles, property of a greater value may be taken without any dishonesty, if the circumstances are such that we are perfectly sure we would have the owner's implied consent. A man once went into a house and took some provisions while the family was away, without doing any wrong. You wonder how this could be. The case was this : he was travelling through the woods and got lost. After wandering about a long time, he came at last upon a farm-house in a solitary place. The family had gone into the field, far away from the house. Now, he knew that if the farmer had been at home, he would willingly have given him some food, as he was almost exhausted by fatigue, hunger and anxiety. So he opened the door and found something to eat ; and then when refreshed a little by food and rest, he went off into the fields to find the farmer, and offered to pay him. But the farmer would not take any pay, saying if he had been at home he would have given him food. So if a man were wrecked with the ship he sailed in, upon a desert island, and he were the only one saved, he might take all the cargo of the ship and use it for his own benefit.

The dishonesty of an act does not consist merely in our taking property that does not belong to us, nor does it depend upon the value of the property; it depends upon our state of mind. Unless we are perfectly sure that the owner would have no objection to our taking it, or if we should feel a little guilty should he come unexpectedly and find us taking it, or if we detect in ourselves a secret wish to conceal from him that we have taken it, — then we are dishonest, no matter how small the value of the article may be. But if we are sure we have the consent of the owner, either expressed or implied, we are not dishonest, no matter how great the value of the article may be.

When it is thus distinctly explained to young people that it is sometimes right to take the owner's consent for granted, they must not presume the consent to be implied when they have no right to do so. It will not do to say, " Oh, I think he will let us have it," and then take things, unless we are sure the owner has no objection to our taking them. Nor is it enough to know that he would let you have it if you asked for it. You must know that he would be willing to let you have it without asking for it. A man who had a large orchard would, no doubt, give apples to boys if they asked him; but it does not follow that he would be willing that boys

should take apples from his orchard without asking.
We must never take what belongs to another, unless we
are quite sure he would be perfectly willing for us to
take it without permission ; as, for instance, raspberries
from his fields, or wild flowers from his meadow, or a
drink of water from his well. These things are all his
property. But we may take them without leave because
it is absolutely certain, not only that he would be willing to give them to us, but also that he would not even
wish us to ask him for them. But when, for any reason
whatever, we have any cause to doubt the owner's consent, then the property must not be taken, whether its
value is great or small ; as, if instead of wild raspberries
from the farmer's field, it is strawberries from his garden
which boys wish to gather, though the value of the fruit
is nearly the same, it may be very right to take the wild
raspberries, and yet very wrong to take the strawberries
from his garden.

3. An honest boy will be honest in fulfilling his
agreements. To fail of fulfilling an agreement, openly
and avowedly, is unjust. To contrive some artful or
secret way of evading what we agreed to do, is dishonest. There are many temptations to dishonesty in
fulfilling agreements for work ; for the man who engages
the workman to do it, very seldom knows exactly how
it ought to be done. He contracts, perhaps, with a
carpenter to build him a house, and he does not know
himself what kind of materials ought to be used for all
the various parts, nor how the work ought to be exe-
cuted. It is so with the painter, the mason, the black-
smith, and all the other trades. Those who work at
them can, in fulfilling their contracts, take advantage of

their employer's imperfect acquaintance with the details of the work. But it is dishonest to do so. A contractor or builder ought to be as faithful as if all the world understood every particular of his work, and could judge of its thoroughness as well as himself. An honest mechanic will do so. He may at first not get so great a profit, but he enjoys a high satisfaction ; his mind is at peace, and he will secure a fine reputation ; while the dishonest workman, for the sake of a little greater gain, wounds his own spirit, and arouses conscience to complaints and murmurings and bitter reproaches, and after a time nobody will trust him.

4. An honest boy is honest in regard to property which some other person has lost, and which he has found, and he endeavors to restore it to the true owner. A dishonest boy does not wish to find the true owner and restore it to him. He wishes to secure it to himself. On some dangerous coasts where vessels are liable to be wrecked, men sometimes go and live in huts on the beach, to be ready to plunder the cargoes and the passengers, as they are driven ashore by the waves. And sometimes they hold out false lights to deceive the sailors. They have no compassion for the unhappy men who barely escape a terrible death, and lose nearly all they have. They only wish to get what is left for themselves. So they leave the suffering people to perish upon the sand, while they rob the passengers and carry away whatever of the cargo they can find. The honest man and honest boy think of the losers when they find what is lost, and do all they can to restore the property to the owner.

QUESTIONS.

What is honesty?

What is property?

Mention some things which we call property.

How may we get property?

How may we lose it?

What are we bound to do with property?

What is the grossest act of dishonesty?

How are thieves universally regarded among men?

What is the second class of dishonest acts called?

Is it possible to avoid having property exposed, so that persons may take it dishonestly if they will?

Is property exposed before children generally? How?

Do children generally think it as wicked to take things from their parents as it would be to steal from other people?

Is there any reason why it should be considered more wicked?

Is it wrong to gain any advantage or pleasure at the expense of other people, without their consent, or to take their property?

Describe the case of the boy going to ride the horse to water.

How can one steal the use of property?

Describe the case of the man who hires a horse to go twenty miles.

What is a boy in danger of becoming, who tries to ride on a car without paying?

What is the meaning of expressed consent?

What is the meaning of implied consent?

Can you mention any case where a person would have an implied consent?

What great danger are children exposed to in regard to this subject?

In what way are mechanics sometimes dishonest in respect to their work?

What does honesty require of us when we find things that have been lost?

FIDELITY.

We must not neglect nor slight the duties we owe to ourselves or others ; but we must do them earnestly and carefully. This is faithfulness or fidelity.

THERE is a difference between honesty and faithfulness which may be illustrated thus : A boy is sent with a basket of fruit, to give to a sick person in the neighborhood. An honest boy will not take any of the fruit himself, but will deliver it safely. But suppose, when he has gone a little way, he should see some other boys playing, and should put his basket down and stop to play with them ; he would be unfaithful. He would not be performing his duty in a thorough and careful manner.

Unfaithfulness often leads to dishonesty. If a boy slights or neglects duty from thoughtlessness, or forgetfulness, or want of care, he is merely unfaithful. If he does so with a secret design to deceive and defraud, he is unfaithful, and dishonest too.

The workmen who attempt to defraud their employers by doing their work in an imperfect and insufficient manner are examples of this. They are unfaithful in their work, and dishonest to their employers.

The distinction may be shown, too, in respect to promises. If we make any promise, secretly intending, when we promise, that we will not perform it, or that we will not perform it well, we are dishonest. Even if

we afterwards do fulfil the promise perfectly, we were
dishonest in making it.   But, on the other hand, if we
make it in good faith, — that is, honestly intending to
keep it, — and afterward from carelessness or design,
neglect the fulfilment, we are unfaithful.   Once a boy
promised his sister that if she would give him a certain
picture-book, he would make her a boat, to sail on the
pond.   She understood him to mean a wooden boat
with masts and sails ; and he intended that she should
understand him so.   But he meant secretly to make her
only a paper boat, which would be good for nothing ;
for as soon as it was set afloat, it would begin to soak
up the water, and very soon turn over or sink.   He was
dishonest in making his promise.   Another boy, however, who promised his sister a boat, really intended to
make one ; but the time passed away and he did not
do it ; other things interested him ; and, though his
sister asked him for her boat many times, he never
made it.   This boy was honest in making his promise,
but unfaithful in keeping it.

The temptation to unfaithfulness is greatest in those
duties or services which are somewhat indefinite in their
nature ; and it is in these that we ought to be particularly on our guard.   If a man agreed to dig a cellar of a
certain size, and to have it done on a certain day, the
engagement would be very distinct and well defined.
If, however, he were to undertake to build a dam across
a stream sufficient for a mill, the engagement would be
more indefinite and vague ; and the temptation to be
unfaithful would be much greater in this last case than
in the other ; because there are many ways of building
a dam, which may have different degrees of strength

and durability; and the man, wishing to do the work with as little labor and expense as possible, would be very likely to think the dam strong when it was really not so. And then, his unfaithfulness could not be so easily and clearly proved against him in this case as in the other. So, if a teacher should give a boy, for a lesson, four examples in arithmetic to do, and should say that when he had got the answers which are given in the book, he might go out to play, it would be a very definite task; and the temptation to unfaithfulness would be comparatively small. But if he were to give him for his lesson two pages of a book, and require him to choose out and study all the difficult words in it, as a spelling lesson, this would be indefinite and vague; because it is very uncertain, first, how many of the words the boy would have to consider as difficult words; and secondly, how much he ought to study them. If the boy was in haste to go out to play, he would be much more likely to slight this lesson than the other one. It is best, therefore, that all commands, and all agreements and contracts, should be well defined, and clearly and distinctly expressed. Thus the temptation to unfaithfulness is lessened. Young people are much exposed to the danger of being unfaithful. It requires, sometimes, much firmness and self-denial to be careful and persevering and thorough in what we do, when there is nobody to see whether we are so or not; and then children are not often aware how great the secret satisfaction is, which we feel when faithful work is done. A boy who is studying at his desk sometimes finds the temptation to be idle and to play very great, if the teacher is occupied with other duties;

but yet, if he studies faithfully, whether he is observed or not, he will have peace and happiness, when the duties of the day are done, which the idle and unfaithful never enjoy.

There is a nobleness in the character of the boy who is strictly faithful in the discharge of his duties. If he goes on steadily and firmly, always the same, whether he is observed by others or not, it shows that he is governed by right principles, which make him worthy of confidence. The farmer's boy, who will work just as industriously whether his father is with him in the field or not, the trusty messenger, who is as careful of the property committed to him as he would be of his own, are characters that are respected and valued by all; while he who does his duty only so long as he is watched, and when left to himself has no principle to sustain him, is suspected and disliked as soon as his character becomes known.

Boys who acquire a character for fidelity enjoy many privileges and advantages which others do not. In fact, very many of the privations and restraints which most boys have to bear are occasioned by the fact that they cannot be trusted. They are not allowed to take a book or tool which they want, because they cannot be depended upon to use it carefully and to bring it back. They are often kept at home when they want to go out, because they cannot be trusted to come back at the proper time. And so, in many ways, they suffer inconvenience and privation just because they are not faithful, and cannot be depended upon. A boy — really faithful — would so gain the confidence of his parents and teachers, that his requests would very seldom be refused.

The advantages of a character for fidelity become still greater when the child grows up to be a man. The most important and desirable situations and employments in life are such as require that those who are appointed to them should be trustworthy. Who would give the command of a ship, or the charge of a manufactory, or the custody of money, or the building of a house, to men who could only be depended upon so long as they are watched ? Unfaithful men are shunned, so far as their characters are known ; while the faithful are sought for and prized, and through the whole of life, in childhood and manhood, they are far more prosperous and happy. A character for fidelity is invaluable ; and the way to establish a character for faithfulness is to be faithful in reality.

QUESTIONS.

What is the difference between honesty and faithfulness?

Is it dishonest or unfaithful to neglect a duty from thoughtlessness?

What is said about promises?

Can a person be honest in making a promise and yet unfaithful in keeping it?

Can he be dishonest in making it and yet faithful in keeping it?

Relate the story of the boy who promised his sister a boat.

In what kind of duties is the temptation to unfaithfulness greatest?

What example is given of an engagement that would be indefinite?

In which case would the temptation to unfaithfulness be the greater?

What examples are given of definite and indefinite lessons?

Are children peculiarly exposed to the danger of being unfaithful?

Do they gain a momentary pleasure by being unfaithful?

Do they do themselves any injury by it? What injury?

What advantages would a child enjoy who was known to be faithful?

Of what advantage is a character for strict fidelity to a man?

JUSTICE.

Justice requires that every person should enjoy all the privileges and rights that are his due ; and we must not do wrong to any one, especially to the weak and defenceless : nor must we encourage wrong-doing by others.

ONE may injure another without being unjust to him ; for injustice is that particular kind of injury to any one which consists in violating his rights. A captain of a ship engages a boy to go with him to sea, to be his cabin-boy, and promises not only to take good care of him, but that he shall not have any severe or dangerous duties to perform. When they are out at sea, and the boy is entirely in the captain's power, he sends him away from the cabin, into the forecastle, with the sailors, some of whom are bad men, and makes him go aloft, and out on the spars, in the dark and stormy nights. This is unjust, for the boy has a right to different treatment ; and the captain in treating him in such a way is depriving him of his rights ; and so is unjust to the boy.

But if, instead of taking the boy from the shore, and agreeing to take care of him, he had found him at sea, upon a wrecked vessel, just ready to perish, and had taken him on board his own ship, then such treatment would not be strictly called unjust. It might be harsh or cruel and it might be very wrong ; but it would not be that particular kind of wrong which is called injustice, because the boy in this case would not have any particular rights on board the captain's ship. There would have been no agreement made with him ; and therefore the captain, in treating him as he did all the other sailors, would not violate any of his rights.

A boy is playing with his ball in a field, and it accidentally gets lodged in a tree, and he asks a larger boy to climb up and get it for him. It is not unjust for the larger boy to refuse to go. He did not lose the ball, and the first boy has no right to call upon him to go and get it. It might be that he ought to go, from a feeling of kindness and good will, still he would violate none of the first boy's rights in refusing ; and therefore, he could not be said to be unjust.

But if the larger boy had been playing with the ball, and had lost it in the tree, then he would be unjust in refusing to climb up and get it ; for the little boy would have a right to require that whoever lost his ball should get it for him again, or at least try to get it. If, therefore, the larger boy should go away, and leave it there, he would be guilty of injustice.

Persons have a variety of rights, and there are many ways by which they may be violated. Very few of these ways can now be particularly explained. We ought to have a strong sense of justice in our hearts, as a settled principle, and then whatever the particular circumstances may be, we shall be ready and willing to act justly. Those who have not such a settled principle are continually encroaching upon the rights of those who are smaller or weaker than themselves, or who are in any way in their power. There are many ways in which this injustice may appear.

1. Young people may be unjust in what they do. They may by some act deprive a brother or playmate of a right or an enjoyment which was properly his, or impose upon him some duty or labor which is more than his share.   A boy was once sent by his father to carry a heavy basket to another house.   His little brother was to go with him to help him.   They put a pole under the handle of the basket, and then they took hold of the pole, one at each end.   While they were getting it ready, the elder boy said to himself, " My little brother don't understand about placing the pole.   If the handle of the basket comes just across the middle of it, then it will be just as heavy for him as for me.   But if I slip the basket over nearer to him, his end will be heavy, and mine will be light ; he will carry more than half of the load, while I carry but little ; and he will not know that there is any difference, for he does not understand about placing the pole.   But yet I will not do so.   I should be unjust if I were to do so ; and I will not be unjust." Then the elder slipped the basket over nearer to his side of the pole ; and so he had to carry more than half. Thus he had a heavier load ; but he had the satisfaction of feeling that he was not unjust ; and that more than made it up to him.

One boy takes a plaything from another and will not give it to him when he asks for it.   He is unjust.   He violates his rights.   Every one has a right to his own property at all times.   A boy knocks another's ball over a fence or wall, or trundles his hoop off down the street, or sets his little boat adrift upon the water.   He is unjust.   He is violating the other's rights.   It is the same spirit which makes men oppressors and tyrants. And yet such cases are very common.

A large boy borrows a ball from a little boy upon the playground, and then keeps it after the owner begs him to give it back to him. When you remonstrate with the large boy for doing so, he says, in excuse, "I was not going to keep his ball; I was going to give it to him again." He admits that it would be very wrong to take away the ball, and keep it for his own use, but seems to think it is not wrong to keep it a little while. But it certainly is wrong. The wrong is of the same kind, and differs only in degree, whether you take away a person's property and keep it from him one hour or keep it forever. So long as you do keep it, after you know he wishes it to be returned, you are guilty of taking what belongs to another. You violate his rights. It is unjust ; it is oppressive.

2. Young people may be unjust in what they say. When we find fault with and condemn the absent, without hearing or considering what they might say in defence of themselves, we are unjust. When we are offended with a companion, and with angry words tell other persons of the wrong he has done, while we conceal or pass over slightly the wrong which we did ourselves, we are unjust. When we complain to a parent or teacher of some injury which a playmate has done us, while we say nothing about the provocation we gave him or the angry words we used, we are unjust. He has a right to claim that, if we tell the story at all, we shall tell it as it was, and not magnify his guilt and pass lightly over our own. If, therefore, we do not state the case fairly and impartially, we violate his rights, and do him injustice.

We may be unjust in what we say to others as well

as in what we say of them. We may get angry with them without a cause, and so reproach them and hurt their feelings when they have not done any wrong. A boy asked his playmate to hold his kite for him till the breeze should come, and then toss it up, while he stood at a little distance with the string. His playmate took the kite, and when the breeze came and the other boy said, "Now," he tossed it up. But the tail got twirled somehow or other around his body and was broken off; the kite rose a little way, and then, having lost its counterpoise, dived to the ground and broke its back-bone. The boy who owned the kite was very angry, and reproached the other bitterly. He was unjust. The breaking of the kite was an accident, for which the boy who tossed it up was not at all to blame. He did as well as he could; and the other wounded his feelings by his harsh language and was guilty of great injustice. It is exceedingly common, both among boys and men, for persons to be vexed and irritated by an accident, and then to do great injustice to those who are innocently the cause of it, by assailing them in violent and angry language.

3. Young people can do injustice by their thoughts. When we hear complaints or accusations against any person, and readily believe them, without knowing what the accused might say in self-defence, we are generally unjust. Even if a person is very much to blame, he will generally appear less to blame, when we understand the case fully, than he did after we had only heard what was said against him. We must therefore be careful, and not judge hastily; and we must not, even in our minds,

condemn the absent unheard. We should not like to be judged and condemned thus ; and it is unjust for us to form opinions in this way about others.

Thus there are many ways by which we may be unjust ; and in all these cases the injustice may be deliberate and wilful, or it may arise from some error or bias of mind of which we are not conscious. Two boys determine to make a summer house in the garden, but cannot agree upon the place to build it, and they refer it to their sister to decide which is the better place, and the older boy tells her secretly that he will give her an apple if she decides in his favor. Now if she does so, while yet the place chosen by the other brother is the better, she is guilty of deliberate, intentional injustice. She knows very well that in deciding in favor of one brother, for the sake of the apple, she is doing injustice to the other ; so, it is a wilful wrong.

But if, on the other hand, no bribe is offered, and if the older boy has been generally more kind to her so that she loves him better, her partiality may blind her judgment, so that she may decide in his favor without being conscious of any intentional injustice toward the other. Our feelings and our wishes do in many ways blind our minds and make us unjust. This is wrong, though it is not deliberate and wilful wrong. We ought to watch ourselves more carefully and be on our guard so as not to be led astray by our own prejudices, or by the representations of others. This kind of injustice is therefore wrong ; though deliberate and intentional injustice is much more criminal, and conscience is generally ready to make it known to us, more or less distinctly, when we are about to treat our companions in an unjust and oppressive manner, in any of these ways.

We are often under a great temptation to be unjust ; but we shall always promote our happiness, as well as do our duty, by resisting it. It is true that we can often gain something by violating the rights of our companions, by taking away some of their enjoyments or imposing upon them more than their share of inconvenience or labor. But those who will make the experiment will find that the satisfaction and happiness of being just, are far greater than any gain we can possibly derive from encroachments upon the rights of others.

QUESTIONS.

Are all kinds of injuries to be considered as injustice?

Relate the case of the captain and the cabin-boy.

Would this be injustice? Why?

Relate the other part of the supposition.

Would this be a case of injustice, strictly speaking? Why?

How is this illustrated by the story of the boys and the ball?

Are there many ways of doing injustice?

Is it possible to describe them all, and make rules against them?

What is the only way by which a person can be preserved from doing injustice?

What is the first of the ways mentioned in which children may be unjust? The second? The third?

Relate the story of the boy and the heavy basket.

Did he act wisely?

How may we be unjust in what we say?

Do you recollect the story told to illustrate this?

Was the boy who tossed up the kite in fault?

What is the meaning of counterpoise?

Do you think it is common for boys to do each other injustice in such ways as this?

How can we be unjust in our thoughts?

Is all injustice deliberate and wilful?

Can a person be unjust and yet not be sensible of it?

Relate the case of the two boys who referred a question to their sister.

What is this intended to show?

POLITENESS.

In school — at work — at play — at home — abroad, we meet with other people ; and we should treat them kindly — not give them pain.

This conduct, when marked by good manners, is politeness.

> " Politeness is to do and say
> The kindest things in the kindest way."

SOCIAL customs are different in every country, but true politeness is the same everywhere. Politeness is good manners, refinement of manners, polish or elegance of manners, good breeding. It is pleasing others by kind and gentle treatment, by anticipating their wants and wishes, and by carefully avoiding giving them pain.

Let us think of politeness as controlling our behavior, at home, at school, in the street, at work, in the cars or steamboats and in church.

AT HOME. It is not polite to interrupt a conversation between persons older than yourself, unless you have something very important to say. It is not good manners.

It is not polite to choose the best seat in the room, or at the table, or near the light in the evening, or near the heat in cold weather.

Say "I thank you," not "thanks," when you are helped to anything, or when any civility or kindness is shown you.

It is not polite to frown or sulk or "answer back," when you are reproved for some neglect or offence.

It is not polite to complain of the quality or the quantity of the food, which is set before you.

AT SCHOOL. Always salute your teacher distinctly when you enter the schoolroom. Do the same to your classmates, even if it be only with a bow or a smile.

A well-bred scholar will give the teacher as little trouble as possible.

Treat your teachers always as you would like to be treated, and ought to be treated, if you were a teacher.

If your teacher seems to be harsh or partial, do not take it for granted that he is so; possibly you are mistaken. Wait a while.

If there are brighter scholars in the class than you, be proud of them, praise them; do not dislike them; try by all fair means to excel them.

IN THE STREET. You have a perfect right to your share of the sidewalk, but to no more than your share. You have no right to stand in a pathway anywhere, so that the people who would pass must go around you. Always give choice of way to women, and to men who are older than yourself.

Never smoke a pipe, a cigar, or a cigarette in the street. It defiles the air. It is not polite to spit on a pavement; if necessary, go to the gutter.

If you are trundling a hoop, or riding on any kind of wheels on a sidewalk, give the right of way to all foot-passengers.

AT WORK. Treat your fellow-workers with respect. Many of them are probably well-bred people; if not, you can help them to be so, by your treatment of them.

Do not try to put any work that belongs to you on others; better take a part of theirs.

Do not be rough in speech or manners, and do not scold harshly one who is under you in any way.

Treat your employers with unfailing respect, and if their character and conduct is such that you cannot safely or properly stay with them, seek employment elsewhere.

IN CARS OR STEAMBOATS. It is not polite to rush for the best seats, nor to occupy more room than you are fairly entitled to. In steam railway carriages you pay for one seat — do not claim two. Do not talk or laugh in such a manner as to attract public attention. If you should smoke tobacco when you grow to be men, do not sit or stand where the wind blows the smoke past other passengers. It is not polite to spit on the floors of cars. You have no right to defile the floor which other people's clothing may touch. It is not polite, it is hardly decent, to be in the habit of spitting in the sight of other people.

IN CHURCH. Be in your seat before the services begin. Do not talk in church. Do not look at your watch during the service. Do not look around the congregation. It is not polite to do these things. Be quiet in church. Be ready to offer your seat and your book to a stranger. Do not use a fan to the annoyance of those near you. If you must fan yourself, do it very gently.

Do not put on your gloves or overcoat until the services are all concluded. After the benediction, be perfectly still for at least a quarter of a minute.

QUESTIONS.

What is politeness?
Where can we show politeness?
Is it polite to interrupt conversation?
May you choose the best place or seat?
May you answer back when rebuked?
Should you treat others as you would be treated?
Is it good manners to obstruct the way of others?
Is it good manners to smoke or spit in public?
Is it better to be rough or gentle?
What is correct behavior in cars or on steamboats?
What are good manners in church?
What is your idea of a polite, well-bred boy or girl?
Is your behavior likely to affect your success in life?

DUTIES AT SCHOOL.

Children at school are under obligation to their parents or guardians to be diligent and faithful in making the best use of their time. They must obey their teachers promptly and cheerfully.

THE first duty for children at school is to be diligent and faithful in improving their time and privileges. There is pleasure in play, and advantage in study. But children make a great mistake in attempting to enjoy the pleasures of play in school hours. There is so much fear of detection, and such constant uneasiness from doing wrong, that playing in school is anything but pleasure. The fears, the anxieties, the forebodings, which necessarily attend it, almost always make it a source of suffering rather than enjoyment.

Even more : idleness in school generally carries its own punishment along with it. Time passes very slowly and heavily to a boy or girl who is idle and listless, waiting for time to pass away, and for close of school. Such a pupil sits restlessly at his seat, now looking out of the window, now counting up how many more classes have yet to recite, and now musing, — his elbow upon his desk, and his cheek upon his hand, — forlorn and miserable. His neighbor, however, in the next seat, is preparing his lesson for the next day. He says to himself, " It is useless to be idle. **Here**

I must stay till school is done. I should like very well to go out to play ; but as I cannot do that, I may as well be employed and forget play." And thus the time passes quickly. So he works diligently upon his next day's lesson, and takes great satisfaction in feeling that he is going on with his duty ; and when at last the bell is struck, he is surprised to find that the time for dismission has come so soon.

It requires an effort — sometimes a great effort — to bring the mind to a state of diligent application ; but if the effort is made, it is at once rewarded by the satisfaction and enjoyment which faithful industry affords. Besides, it is very wrong to waste or misimprove the privileges which are provided for children. Parents and teachers know the value of education, and they wish to secure it for those who are now in the schools.

Children are bound to submit with cheerfulness to all the requirements of their teachers, as to their studies and conduct in school. Children cannot choose their studies. The teacher will establish rules which the pupil sometimes thinks unnecessary or too strict. But it is of no consequence if he does think so. The teacher must decide. A pupil should never put his opinion or his will in opposition to that of the teacher. He must reflect that when he grows up, it may be his time to command. But now it his duty to obey.

In almost all schools there are some dull pupils, who are unprincipled in character as well as weak in intellect, who busy themselves in tricks and roguery. They do all they can to lead better boys to practise the same things ; and they contrive plans for making difficulties, disturbing the order of the school, and giving the teacher trouble. If there can be any satisfaction in disturbing the teacher's peace and happiness, they certainly get it, for nothing is more likely to give a teacher pain, than to find any pupils in a state of deliberate and wilful hostility to the authority of the school. Such characters are to be shunned, and their guilty practices to be discountenanced and discouraged in every way. If they find that the intelligent and the good altogether disapprove of their course, they may perhaps abandon it and return to their duty.

Do not trouble the teacher with frivolous complaints about other pupils, or be a tale-bearer to carry stories of their misconduct. If the teacher does anything which you think is wrong, do not tell the story exultingly and with exaggeration. Remember, when you speak of the teacher or of the pupils away from school, that they are not present to hear your accusations, and to excuse, explain, or defend their conduct. You must be very careful, therefore, not to do them injustice. State everything fairly, just as it is, and mention all the favorable as well as the unfavorable circumstances. We ought never to accuse or censure the absent, unless peculiar circumstances render it necessary or unavoidable ; and then we ought to be very careful lest we do them injustice.

While children should be very unwilling and slow to speak of the faults of others, yet, when they are required by a parent or teacher to give information in regard to any wrong that has been done, they should do what witnesses are sworn to do, when they give evidence in courts of justice : they should state all that they know, promptly, fully, and with exact justice to all concerned. It is dishonorable to be constantly making complaints of others for the sake of getting favor to one's self; and it is always so considered. Such a person is an informer, a tale-bearer. But to make honest statements of facts, when required to do so by the proper authorities, is honorable and praiseworthy; and this is universally so considered among men. It is giving testimony. No gentleman refuses to do it, when called upon the stand in court; and no child ought to make any difficulty in doing it, when he, too, is called upon by those who have a right to make the demand.

It undoubtedly requires firmness and decision to resist all the various temptations which occur at school, and to be at all times diligent, faithful, and persevering, in fulfilling the duties which arise there. But when good habits are formed, it will be easy to continue them; and the effort which it is necessary to make, will be richly rewarded by the great advantages which they will bring in future life.

QUESTIONS.

What is the first duty of a child at school?
Is it pleasant to be idle in school hours?
Does it make the time seem shorter or longer to be busy?
What did the industrious boy say to himself?
Do children always like to do what their teachers direct?
Ought they to obey the rules whether they approve them or not?
Ought they to obey good-humoredly?
How may children treat their teachers unjustly?
Is it right to tell the faults of other scholars?
When it is required by the teacher, how should it be done?
Should unkind tales of other scholars be repeated out of school?

DUTIES TO PLAYMATES.

When with playmates, we must avoid those who are vicious ; we must encourage those who do right; we must discourage those who do wrong, and protect the weak and defenceless. We must promote good feeling, and be kind to all.

1. One of the most important things for boys to consider, as to their playmates, is to avoid the company of the vicious. The vicious are such as lie, cheat, steal, and use profane and corrupt words. If a boy goes into a new neighborhood, or comes to a new school, or is thrown among boys whom he did not know before, he will soon learn who are the vicious. They will betray themselves by their language, or be openly unjust and oppressive to the smaller boys, or they will have some plan for deceiving the teacher, and, perhaps, will propose to the other boys to join them in a deliberate lie. Whenever you discover such a character as this, avoid him. Be civil when you meet him, but have as little to do with him as possible. You must be especially on your guard if you find that he tries to keep your company, or wants you to go with him. Be firm and resolute in avoiding him. If not, he will probably make you as bad as himself.

2. Always try to encourage doing right, and to discourage doing wrong, among your playmates, by every means in your power. Boys are very often led to do what is wrong, by knowing that other boys are looking

on and approving what they do. Bystanders, who thus encourage others in doing wrong, share the guilt of it. They are accomplices. A boy was once led to throw stones at the back windows of the schoolhouse and break the glass, by the influence of boys, who stood by, and dared him to do it. So, if one man is breaking into a house in the night, and another holds the light for him, and a third stands doing nothing, but yet consenting to the deed, and another acts as a sentinel to prevent dis-covery, they are all alike guilty. If a circle of boys gather around two, who are quarrelling or fighting, and look on with interest and gratification, they all partake of the wrong-doing. A true, manly boy will not do this. If he sees anything wrong, or hears anything wrong pro-posed, he will discourage and prevent it if he can; and if not, he will go away. He will not countenance, by his presence, anything which his conscience condemns.

3. Always try to protect the weak and defenceless, and to help all who are in any difficulty or trouble. We might suppose that no one would degrade himself so much, as to be guilty of cruelty and oppression to those who are younger and smaller than himself. But there are boys who will do this. Their consciences, however, condemn them while they do it; and the influence of the good opinion of others will sometimes keep them from doing wrong. They know it is wrong, and if the other boys condemn it, they will often refrain from doing it. By taking part with the oppressed, it is often possible to diminish very much the oppression; and there are many other ways by which a just and conscientious boy may help to protect his playmates from injury.

4. Promote peace and good will among your play-mates. A boy may do much to secure harmony among his companions, by explaining misunderstandings, by representing things that occur, in a favorable light, and, by being an example of kindness and good nature, in all his conversation and conduct. On the other hand, he may do much to cause discord and ill will, by trying to set one boy against another, by repeating harsh things which have been said, by exaggerating difficulties and misunder-standings, and by indulging, and encouraging others to indulge a revengeful and a passionate spirit. One of the most common ways of causing ill will, both among children and grown persons, is, when we hear anything said in ridicule or censure of an absent person, to go and tell him of it, and thus exasperate him against the person who said it. This is very wrong. We never should repeat what is likely to produce ill will, unless some peculiar circumstances render it necessary. Some persons do it on purpose to make difficulty. They go to one person and tell him what severe things another has said of him. Then they go to the other, and make the same complaint to him against the first, — exaggerating, and perhaps wholly inventing, the things which they say they have heard. Such a character is a tale-bearer. We must never listen to a tale-bearer when he comes to tell us unkind stories about others. We must be very careful also, not to speak ill of persons absent, so as to give any tale-bearer who may hear, an opportunity to repeat our words to them, and make them angry. And, in all our own conversation with our companions, we must endeavor to soften their angry feelings and make them excuse the faults of others ; and we must care-

fully suppress and conceal all that would tend to alienate one of our playmates from another, and produce secret ill will, or, perhaps, open quarrels.

5. Young people should be courteous to one another in their manners. Boys ought to be gentlemanly, and girls ladylike, in all their conversation and demeanor. There is every reason for this. It is proper in itself. Politeness is only gentleness and kindness expressed in our manners and conversation. Gentleness and kindness are agreeable; they promote happiness; while a rude, rough, and ill-natured manner makes others uncomfortable. All sharp and hasty words, quick contradictions, eager selfishness about little things, struggles for the best seats and best places, taunting and uncivil questions, rude answers, and all loud, rough, and boisterous conduct, in the presence of grown persons, in the house or anywhere else, — all such manners are rude and unbecoming. They disturb the peace and happiness of others; and whoever wishes to be conscientious in duty, will be careful to form very different habits of conduct.

Two boys are running to overtake their companions, and they come to a stone wall where there is only one good place to climb over. They rush together for the gap. They scramble and crowd into it, each pulling back the other. The stronger boy prevails. He throws the other back among the fallen stones, and then dashes through, and runs on, leaving his playmate behind, bruised, vexed, and unhappy.

Two other boys come up to the gap in the wall under the same circumstances. The elder, with instinctive politeness, slackens his pace an instant, to let the other pass over before him. Small boys never like to be behind in overcoming a difficulty. It makes them anxious, and afraid that they will be left behind. The elder therefore helps his young companion through, and then follows; then they run on, both in undisturbed fun. The politeness has wasted no time; it has diminished no pleasure; it has caused no pain. And so it always is. Politeness and kind consideration for others, smooth the roughness of play, overcome difficulties and heighten enjoyment. They bind playmates together in strong bonds of affection, and form in boys and girls such manners and habits, as make them objects of regard and affection while they are young, and secure for them great advantages, when they grow up, in their intercourse with the world at large.

QUESTIONS.

In choosing playmates, whom must we avoid?

What are vicious boys?

How do vicious boys generally show their characters?

What effect is the acquaintance of a vicious boy likely to have?

In what way ought a boy to use his influence over his playmates?

If a boy encourages another to do wrong, does he not share in the guilt of it?

How is this illustrated by the case of the broken windows?

Suppose you know of a wrong about to be done, and you cannot prevent it, what must you do?

What is the third direction given in the lesson?

Do cases of oppression and cruelty often occur among boys?

Can good boys do anything to prevent it? How?

Can a boy do anything to promote peace among his playmates? In what way?

Can he do anything to promote dissension and ill will? In what way?

Do these principles apply to girls as well as boys?

Did you ever know boys or girls to take pleasure in telling their playmates the evil which others have said of them?

Is this right or wrong? What harm does it do?

What is meant by being courteous?

Describe the cases of the boys and the stone wall.

BENEVOLENCE.

It is our duty to do good to other people and make them happy. This is benevolence. Doing intentionally anything that gives other people pain, without just cause, is malice.

MALICE is very hateful. We must not suppose, however, that in every case where a person causes suffering to another, there is malice. It is not malicious unless he intends to make others suffer. Two boys go down to the water, to sail a toy boat. It is at a place where the road passes along by the shore, and where the water is shallow, and the bottom is sandy, so that travellers can drive their horses in a little way to let them drink. The boys play with their boat until at last it gets out beyond their reach, and they do not know what to do.

Now, suppose a gentleman and a lady should come along in a carriage, busily engaged in talking, and should drive into the water, and run over the boat, letting the horses trample it down, because they would not take the trouble to turn aside ; and then the gentleman were to say, " There, boys, we've run over your boat ; but you'd no business to have it in the way." This would be harsh ; but it would not be malicious. It would only be a selfish disregard of the happiness of others. The gentleman did not particularly wish to run over the boat, but he did not take pains to avoid it.

But, suppose a rough boy were to come along on foot,

and, seeing the boat floating away, should take up stones to throw at it; and, after throwing several times, should succeed in hitting it and breaking it to pieces; and then should go away, laughing at the sorrow and distress which the children would feel. This would be malicious.

And, again, suppose instead of the malicious boy on foot, two boys were to come along in a wagon, and, seeing the boat out upon the water, should say to the children, "Can't you get back your boat?" and when the children say, "No," suppose they were to cut a long stick, and drive in as far as they could go safely, and then reach out with the stick, and carefully draw the boat to the shore. This would be benevolent.

Suppose another man were to drive over the boat, without seeing it, and then, after his horse had finished drinking, were to drive on, without knowing that he had done any mischief. This would not be benevolent, nor malicious, nor selfish. It would be merely an accident, and worthy of no praise, and of no blame.

Thus we may injure others accidentally; or we may injure them because we do not care about their happiness, but only wish to secure our own ends, — which is selfishness; or we may injure them intentionally, for the sake of giving them pain, and gratifying bad passions by seeing them suffer; this is malice. Malice is always hateful. But it is not always malicious to do a person an injury; and we must, therefore, when harm is done to us, consider the case calmly, and not charge a person who injures us with being malicious, unless the case is such as to prove that he really is so.

There is some distinction to be made in regard to acts of kindness and benevolence. If we do good to others accidentally, or without a design to do them good, it is not benevolence; as, for instance, where a gardener threw the cuttings and trimmings of the garden in a heap, and a boy found some rose-bush shoots, with little roots, among them, and set them out; and where a man overflowed his meadow, to kill the alders, and thus made a fine skating-ground for the boys. He intended, it is true, to overflow his meadows, but he did not intend any advantage to the boys by it. Therefore it was not benevolent.

And even when we do intend to benefit other persons by what we do, if our object, in the end, is to benefit ourselves, it is not benevolence. A man wants to have his horse watered, and, having no other convenient way, tells a boy who lives near him that he may ride him down to the stream, and let him drink. Now, although the man knows very well that the boy would like to go, yet, if his object is, not to give the boy the gratification of a ride, but only to get his horse watered, then there is no benevolence in the action. Most men, in such cases, are influenced by both motives; and thus the action is, in part, a benevolent one.

When one does what seems to be benevolent, while yet his real intention is to gain some good for himself, he may be doing right or he may be doing wrong; it depends upon circumstances. But, right or wrong, it is not benevolence. As malice, or malevolence, consists in doing evil for the purpose of gratifying bad passions, by making persons suffer, so benevolence consists in doing good for the purpose of making them happy. The latter is excellent and lovely; the former is to be abhorred.

To tease, or torment, the weak and defenceless — make them unnecessary trouble, or give them pain — is malicious. Wounding their feelings, by ridiculing them, or calling them nicknames, or terrifying them by threats of violence, to gratify our own bad passions, or to make amusement for ourselves or others, is malicious. So is every mode of worrying or torturing the poor defenceless animals, that cannot speak to remon· strate against our cruelty, or beg to be spared, — all this is malicious. It is one of the darkest traits that the human character can assume. So far as it prevails at the school, upon the playground, or at home, it makes misery. It destroys peace ; it banishes smiles ; and it clouds the face with an expression of suffering and sorrow. It promotes revenge, hatred, mutual ill will, and continual strife. It is detestable.

On the other hand, kindness and good will carry a charm with them wherever they go. Even in little things, where good feeling shows itself only in pleasant words and gentle looks, it is like sunshine, which gladdens every group and every scene that it falls upon. A good-natured and obliging boy, who will be ready to help those who are in difficulty ; to protect the defenceless and the oppressed ; to share his enjoyments with his playmates, and to speak in a kind and gentle manner to all, — one such boy sometimes diffuses happiness over a whole school, or a whole neighborhood ; and if the world were filled with such people, a very happy world it would be.

QUESTIONS.

What is benevolence?

What is malice?

When one person occasions suffering to another, is it always malicious?

What is essential in order to make it so?

Relate the case of the children and the boat.·

Who came there first, and what did they do?

Was this malicious?

Did they wish to do any injury to the boat?

Who came next, — on foot? What did he do?

Did he intend to destroy the boat?

Was this malice?

Did the suffering of the children give him pain, or amuse him?

Who came in a wagon?

What did they do?

What kind of conduct was this?

Did it pain or amuse these boys to see the children suffer from the loss of their boat?

Is it likely the boat was a valuable one?

Would that make any difference in regard to the character of the transactions?

How might the boat have been injured accidentally?

Suppose a person does some good to others, for the sake of gaining some object of his own: is that benevolence?

What influence does a malicious boy exert upon those connected with him?

What influence does a kind and benevolent boy or girl exert?

Do you sometimes observe malicious character and conduct among boys and girls?

Do you sometimes observe kind and benevolent acts?

DUTIES TO DUMB CREATURES.

The birds of the air, the fish of the sea, the animals that creep or walk on the earth, were made for man's use, and are more or less under his power. They cannot speak, and their defenceless condition is an appeal for kind treatment.

THERE are at least three reasons why we should treat dumb creatures kindly.

1. FOR THE SAKE OF THE CREATURE ITSELF. Do not make it wretched. Cruelty to dumb creatures and cruelty to children are alike in kind; it is the strong oppressing the weak, aggravated in the case of dumb creatures, for they cannot complain, they cannot defend themselves, and they do not revenge their wrongs. If dumb creatures could talk, we would not be so likely to be cruel to them.

2. FOR OUR OWN SAKE. One who is tender and compassionate in his feelings will not confine his pity to man alone, but will pity dumb creatures also. A boy who is cruel to dumb creatures will, unless he is changed, become cruel to any persons under him. The feelings become blunted and hardened; the tendency is toward the savage.

3. FOR GOD'S SAKE. The Bible abounds in references to the dumb creatures. "A righteous man regardeth the life of his beast." "Thou shalt not muzzle the ox that treadeth out the corn." "Doth God care for the

oxen?" "Not even a sparrow falleth to the ground without your Heavenly Father," etc.

A boy of twelve years was driving a pair of very small oxen on the shore of a bay of salt water. It was a warm day in May, and the oxen were tired and thirsty. Seeing the water, and not knowing it to be salt, they broke from the little driver's control, and rushed into the water to drink; but they could not drink salt water. The boy beat them over the head with his rough stick and soon brought them under control again. A gentleman who saw it, talked with the boy, who was angry, and tried to show him how cruel it was to beat the oxen, for they only tried to get water; and especially he told the boy of the danger of beating them over the head, lest he should hurt their eyes and make them blind. The boy took the advice kindly; he had never been talked to about it before; he promised not to do so again.

One of the best things the English author Sterne ever wrote, was the incident of Uncle Toby and the fly. The fly had been buzzing about Uncle Toby's face and head during dinner, until he was compelled to catch it. The first impulse was to crush it, but the kindly old man did a better thing. He rose from the table, opened the window and threw it out, saying, "Go, poor thing, get thee gone; there is room enough in the world for thee and me both."

In London there is a hospital or refuge for homeless, friendless dogs, where they are saved from starvation; and if not found to be of any value, or not called for by owners, they are put to death without pain. All honor to the people who establish and support such an asylum.

There are places in other cities where sick and

wounded cats and dogs are received and treated with much care and tenderness, and a great University has prepared a place where sick horses and other animals may be cared for.

Much of the cruelty which is inflicted on dumb creatures is from thoughtlessness and indifference. Little children will worry and vex young kittens and dogs, not knowing how much pain they give. Boys who drive cattle, use heavy sticks which bruise the flesh. A boy driving a cart will use the heavy end of his whip on the horse or mule. The driver of a street car will beat a horse if he slips or stumbles. A refinement of cruelty is to rein up a horse by a kind of bridle, which compels him to hold up his head to a painful and unnatural height. Street cars are too often overloaded, and the suffering to which the horses are thus subjected is deplorable.

Rabbits and other animals, by the hundreds, are tortured by medical students in order to learn what has been learned often before by other students, the results of which have been published. This is called vivisection. The poor, helpless, dumb creatures are tortured by man for his profit, in his passion, or in the name of science.

Cruelty to dumb creatures has become such an admitted fact, that societies have been formed for its prevention, whose agents look after animals and punish people who ill-treat them. Much of this ill-treatment is due to thoughtlessness; but the want of thought is itself wrong, and ought to be corrected. An idle boy at school digs with a penknife a hole in the top of his desk, then fits a little piece of glass in it, and catches and imprisons flies in it to perish. Boys sometimes catch flies and stick pins through them, and so fasten them to a board or desk; or pull off their wings or legs. Boys tease and worry cats, and sometimes stone them to death. Some boys carry gum-elastic slings (sling-shots) to shoot pebbles at birds. This causes suffering and sometimes death to living creatures, for no other purpose than the excitement of learning to shoot accurately.

It is quite common to put up pigeons in a coop and gather a company of sportsmen for practice in shooting. The birds are let loose, and the gunners fire at them as they fly. Killed and wounded, they fall to the ground, and records are kept of the successful shooting. Can anything be more cruel? There is not even the excuse that the birds are killed for food; it is only for sport. An exhibition of this kind was once made on a large scale. Thousands of pigeons were killed, wounded, and crippled by men who shot at them for the purpose of ascertaining who could kill, wound, and cripple the greatest number. The prize was a diamond badge, and the winner was called a champion, precisely as if he had performed some notable feat. Champions of this sort ought to go to jail. The dumb beasts, as well as human beings, are God's creatures. He made them all; He cares for them all.

The hunter shoots and wounds the squirrel. The poor creature creeps to its hole, lies writhing in agony, and finally dies a lingering, painful death. How little the gunner thinks or cares for this! How do we know but that

> " the poor beetle that we tread upon.
> In corporal suffering feels a pang as great
> As when a giant dies?"

Some young men go to a livery stable, hire a horse and carriage, and go off to a tavern, get drunk, and drive the horse until he drops dead. A man overworks a horse in a cart; the wheel gets into a rut; the horse is unable to pull it out, but he cannot say so, and the man falls to beating him, not with a whip, but with a heavy stick, or bludgeon. The horse cannot defend himself; he cannot even complain of this cruel treatment.

There are vicious people who train chickens and dogs for fighting. We call this brutal. It is not the proper word; the brutes are better than this.

To do wrong or to hurt one who is younger or weaker than ourselves is the act of a coward, and any one who needlessly hurts a dumb creature is a coward. It is a serious offence to call a person a coward, but it is not too harsh a word to apply to one who ill-treats a helpless dumb creature.

By common consent many dumb animals are claimed by man for food, and the claim generally is not questioned; but we cannot eat them alive, so we put them to death. This, however, should be done as quickly and with as little pain as possible. Fish, when caught for food, should not be allowed to die slowly gasping for their natural element, but should be killed promptly. Young people should not be permitted or encouraged to be present when animals are put to death. It is for this reason that people having the care of boys, in seeking suitable work for them, will not willingly have them taught the trade of a butcher, however necessary that occupation may be, lest the sight of blood and of death should be hurtful to the young mind.

QUESTIONS.

What are dumb creatures?

How many reasons for treating them kindly?

What are they?

What is the story of the boy and the oxen?

Tell the story about Uncle Toby.

Are there hospitals for sick animals?

Mention some ways in which people are cruel to animals.

Is it right or wrong to have shooting-matches?

What about fishing?

Should we fish for sport simply?

Is it brave or cowardly to hurt those who are younger or weaker than we are?

What is it when a dumb creature is abused?

When animals are killed for food, how should it be done?

TREATMENT OF ENEMIES.

If we have enemies, we ought not to do them evil; but so far as it is in our power, we ought to do them good. If we cannot do them good, we must bear their enmity with a patient and forgiving spirit. This is best for us, and best for our enemies; and it is a duty which God requires.

An enemy is one who wilfully does us an injury. If a boy gives pain or suffering to another accidentally, he is not his enemy. If a parent punishes a child, and thus gives him pain, the parent is not on this account the child's enemy; for his design is to do good, and not evil. Enmity is a feeling which leads one to desire to do evil to another, not because it is necessary in order to accomplish some good object, but to gratify hatred or revenge.

A person may do an injury to others, not for the sake of injuring them, but to gain some advantage himself. In such a case, he is not, strictly speaking, their enemy. If some boys were to get into an orchard to steal the fruit, they would not be, on this account, the owner's enemies; for their motive is only to obtain the fruit for themselves; they do not particularly wish to do the owner any injury. They have no feelings of enmity and ill will towards him. If there were apple-trees growing in the road, they would as readily take them there, as go into the orchard for them. So they are not his enemies.

But if some boys, hating the man for any cause, were to go into the orchard to break down the branches of the trees, not to do themselves any good, but only to do the owner injury, then they are his enemies. Their motives are resentment and ill will. If there were trees in the road, it would not satisfy them at all to break them down, for their special object is to do this man an injury.

It is plain, then, that it is wrong for any person to be another's enemy. Sometimes it is necessary to give other persons pain, but it is always wrong to do this wilfully and intentionally, and with hostile feelings. Parents and teachers are compelled sometimes to inflict pain upon children, as punishment; in such cases, however, their object is not suffering itself, but the good which they hope the suffering will be the means of accomplishing. In punishing children and pupils in a proper manner and with a proper spirit, they who punish are friends of the children, and not their enemies. There are many other ways by which persons may give pain, without being moved to do so by malice or ill will. But if a person is actuated by feelings of malice and ill will, when he gives any other person pain, for the sake of giving pain, he is always wrong. We ought to do good to others, and not evil. We ought to desire to make them happy, not to see them suffer.

When other persons do evil to us, with hostile intentions, the first impulse is to repay them by doing evil to them. If a man injures his neighbor in any way, and if his neighbor injures him in return, this is retaliation.

It might at first be supposed that retaliation would

have a good effect in preventing the enemy who injures us once from doing so again. If he finds that every time he does anything to cause us pain, we retaliate, he will learn, we might suppose, that he always brings injury upon himself by attempting to injure us, and thus that he would soon be compelled to cease. We might suppose that this would be the effect; but when we come to see what the effect really is, we find it is very different. A bad boy gets some stones together to throw at me, when I am going to school. If I throw stones at him as I pass along, instead of making him give up such hostile acts afterwards, it only encourages him to collect more stones for the next day. It makes him a greater enemy than before, — more hostile, more malicious, more bent on doing evil than ever.

But, as I pass along the street the next day, I see that boy carrying something very heavy in a basket, and I go to him and say, " Let me help you carry it a little way," — and take hold with him and carry it along, — it is very probable that, after that, he will not throw any more stones. Retaliation makes his hostility greater; showing him kindness makes it less, or takes it away. If I do evil to him, I make it more probable that he will try hereafter to do evil to me. If I do him good, I am almost certain to prevent him from ever trying to injure me again.

This is one reason why our Saviour said, " Love your enemies ; do good to them that hate you." He saw that this was a far better way than retaliation, to protect ourselves from future injuries. But there is another reason, which is, perhaps, stronger still. And that is, that doing good to our enemy is not only better for us, but it is very much better for him. The angry and malicious feelings in his heart are very wrong, and make him miserable, and we must not do anything to increase them. If we can in any way make him give up such feelings, and cherish friendliness and good will towards us, we make him a great deal happier, as well as ourselves.

A man lived in a village where there were two or three bad boys ; and one of them, who had become displeased with him in some way or other, one evening broke the glass in a window which opened into a toolroom. The man caught the boy, and held him until he saw who it was, and then let him go, so that he might have time to consider what he should do. As he was considering, he said to himself, " I could easily have whipped the boy for breaking my window, but that would not have prevented him from breaking my windows again ; it would probably have made him only more secret about it. Besides, to keep my windows from being broken is not the most important thing. His heart is in a very wrong and wretched state. Now, if I can change the character of his feelings, I shall do him a great deal of good. And it is much more important for him that this should be done, than it is for me to prevent his breaking any more of my windows."

Some days after this, the man was going towards home, and he overtook this boy, who was walking before him. It was winter, and the man was riding in a sleigh. He stopped his horse and asked the boy to get in and ride with him. The boy felt ashamed when he saw who it was, and at first refused to get in ; but the man insisted upon it so strongly and with so good-humored an air and manner, that he got in. But he trembled and was afraid, expecting that he would have to receive very severe rebukes for breaking the window.

Instead of reproaching him, or saying anything whatever to him about his fault, the man said, "If you like to drive, take the reins and the whip, and drive me into the town." The boy did like to drive very much indeed. So he drove into the town, and when he got pretty near his own house, they stopped, and he got out, and said, "Good by, sir. I am much obliged to you for my ride; and I am very sorry indeed that I broke your window."

The excellence of this way of managing such a case, does not arise so much from the fact that it was a very good way to prevent the boy from breaking any more windows, but that it had so good an influence upon the boy's mind, in making him ashamed of his bad passions. Retaliation would only have exasperated him. Just punishment, inflicted by his father or teacher, or by any one who was authorized to punish him, might have done him good; but anything from the man whom he had injured, of the nature of retaliation and revenge, would only have exasperated him. This free forgiveness softened and subdued him. Revenge would have strengthened the bad feeling which was in his mind. Forgiveness removed it.

Whenever, therefore, we find that we have enemies, and it is in our power to do them either good or evil, as we may choose, it is our duty to do them good. But sometimes the circumstances may be such, that it seems not to be in our power either to injure them or to do them good; as when a young boy comes to a school

where there is a large boy who takes pleasure in oppressing him and in giving him pain, by every means in his
power. This is sometimes called hazing. The young
boy is too weak to retaliate upon the one who thus
injures him, even if he desires to do so. And, on the
other hand, day after day passes, without bringing any
opportunity to do him good. The poor boy's oppressor
is above his reach and beyond his power. What shall
he do in such a case as this?

There is nothing for him to do but to be patient,
taking care to avoid his guilty tormentor as much as
he can, and bear with a quiet spirit what he cannot
escape. This forbearance and gentleness will do much
more to subdue hostility than any angry resistance; and
even if it would not, still it is our duty to exercise it.
There is very much oppression and iniquity in this world
for which there is no remedy, and the innocent are often
hopelessly held in the power of the wicked. It is in
such cases useless as well as wrong, to allow our minds
to become irritated and vexed, and to struggle in fruit-
less anger against evils which we cannot overcome, and
which, therefore, must be borne. Let us always bear
wrong done to ourselves with a patient and submissive
spirit as long as we possibly can.

We must be very careful not to think that any persons are our enemies when they are really not so. A
person who is very ready to believe, without any good
reason, that other persons are wishing to injure him,
causes himself unnecessary pain. He is always suspicious and distrustful. Sometimes we imagine from a
person's countenance that he dislikes us, or we inter-
pret some action which was really innocent as a sign

of hostility. A girl went to school one day, and found several girls talking together in a corner, and the expression of their countenances indicated displeasure. So she concluded at once that they were saying something against her, and she was very much offended. But it was without any reason whatever; for they were really talking about something else, and had just finished what they had to say, when she came in; and so just at that moment they stopped talking and got up and went away.

We ought to consider the conduct of others as favorably as we can, and above all things never to think that they are hostile to us, without clear and positive evidence. It has very often happened that two persons have gradually got into a serious quarrel, from no cause whatever, except that each was unreasonably suspicious of the other. In such a case if both, besides being suspicious, have a spirit of retaliation, the difficulty soon becomes irreconcilable. For the spirit of retaliation always leads on from bad to worse.

We see then that the way to treat our enemies and all who show any ill will or hostility to us, is this : —

1. If those who injure us are in any way in our power, we must use that power to do them good and not evil. A spirit of good will and forgiveness will not only be best for us, but it will be best for those who injure us; as it is exactly calculated to make them sorry for the wrong which they have done, and unwilling to repeat it.

2. If those who injure us are not in our power, and if we cannot do them good or evil in return for their injuries, then we must bear patiently and quietly what

we cannot prevent. If we become vexed and irritated against those who show this hostility, we increase our own sufferings, and perhaps make our enemies worse than before.

3. We must not be jealous and suspicious, but always ready to put the most favorable construction upon what we observe in others. We ought to suppose that their feelings are friendly, until we have the most positive proof that they are not ; and we must always treat them with kindness and good will, even if we have good cause to doubt the kindness and good will which they render to us in return.

QUESTIONS.

What is an enemy?

Is any one who does us an injury accidentally, our enemy?

If any one gives us pain with a design to do us good, is he an enemy?

What example of an enemy is given?

What was the case supposed in respect to the boys stealing the farmer's apples?

Were they, strictly speaking, his enemies?

What is the case supposed in which they would be his enemies?

Is it ever right for us to be the enemy of any person?

What is the first impulse which people generally feel when any one does them an injury?

What is this called?

Does retaliation do any good?

Does it do any injury? What injury?

Relate the story of the boy who broke the window.

Suppose the person who is injured has no power to do the one who injures him either good or evil: what is his duty?

Do such cases often occur among boys?

Can you state the general rules given at the end of the lesson?

PROFANITY.

In common conversation and in anger, we often hear the name of God used irreverently. It is taking His name in vain, and it is wicked. This is profanity.

THE habit of profane swearing is a most detestable one, and adds no force to language. It is very common among boys, even very young boys. The mind easily catches that which is evil, and retains it in the memory. The habit of swearing, if acquired in boyhood, is apt to cling to one all through life. Many men are so careless of their example, that they swear in the presence of young boys, who, unless they are on their guard, will quickly form the habit also. There seems to be an impression that seamen especially are excusable for swearing; and it has been said that common sailors will not do their best work unless the officer swears at them. But there are sea-captains who do not swear in giving their orders; and it is not true that an order which is given with an oath has more force and is more likely to be obeyed.

There are many persons so unwilling to take the name of God on their lips, except in worship, that they will not take the judicial oath before a magistrate, but make a solemn affirmation. We must have high respect for such persons, even if we do not adopt their method. Profanity is one of the most vulgar,

vicious, and wicked of all vices.   There is absolutely
no reason or justification for it.   "Other sins offer at
least some appearance of pleasure, or some poor excuse
of temptation : this sin of swearing offers none."[1]   Men
say they do it thoughtlessly and do not mean anything
by it.   Boys take it up because they hear men swear,
and they think it is manly.   It is not manly ; it is mean.
Nothing is more awful than to hear from thoughtless,
flippant lips, the name of Jesus Christ uttered as an oath.
And when such words come from the lips of a boy, they
are appalling.   Would any boy dare to swear in the presence of his mother ?   How very unreasonably wicked
it is for men or boys to cultivate or indulge habits of
speech so immoral, that no lady could properly imitate
them !   And how low and degrading is this vice of
profane swearing !   It is the language of low and
ill-bred people.   The use of it always lowers one in
the estimation of those whose good opinion is worth
having.

There are few habits into which a boy may fall, so
utterly ruinous to him, as the use of profane language.
It seems to destroy the fine sensibilities, the best affec-
tions and generous feelings.   Such a boy knows that
he is doing something which is wrong, something he is
afraid to have his parents and best friends know, and
he loses that frankness and open-heartedness which a
manly boy enjoys.

This vice seems to lead to other vices.   It deadens
conscience, and makes one so reckless of everything
that is delicate and high-minded, that the profane boy

[1] Farrar.

is very likely to grow to be a rough, coarse man. Very probably he will add other vices to this, such as drinking, gambling and other kinds of dissipation.

The influence of this wicked practice is so destructive of everything estimable in character, that a boy who is in the habit of profanity is not a fit companion for other boys, and should be banished from the playground and the school. He is contaminating every one who associates with him.

God's name may be taken in vain by the irreverent repeating of a prayer, or by thoughtless trifling in singing a hymn or saying a grace at table.

There is such a thing as profanity without spoken words. One may swear in his mind without speaking. There is much of this kind of swearing when people are in a passion, or under some high provocation. Now this is not quite so bad as spoken words, because the evil is confined to the person who has such thoughts; but it is a great sin against God, and the stain of every such thought is left on the mind, and cannot easily be erased. You cannot take a live coal in your hand and not be burned; you cannot touch pitch and not be defiled. Avoid this most senseless of all vices; and if any boy has unfortunately fallen into it already, let him break it off, no matter what it costs him. Otherwise, his example may be eagerly copied by those who are younger than he, and he will do much evil by the indulgence of this most pernicious habit.

When the American army were at their winter-quarters in New Jersey, during the Revolutionary War, General Washington one day invited his staff-officers to dine with him. The use of profane language was then very common among the officers of the army. One of them uttered an oath at the table. General Washington suddenly laid his knife and fork upon the table in such a way as to attract the attention of every guest, and raising his hands, exclaimed, "I really thought that I had invited none but gentlemen to dine with me." The reproof was of course deeply felt, and exerted a very great influence in checking the vulgar and despicable vice.

Remember that God hears every word you say; and you cannot give utterance to a profane or indelicate word, without destroying the delicacy of your feelings and paving the way to ruin. And what a terrible thought it is that a child would never swear if it did not hear other people swear! What an awful sin lies on the consciences of those who swear in the presence of children, knowing full well that those children will themselves swear, when they are not afraid of being punished! How can a father punish his boy for profanity when he is himself profane?

> "It chills my heart to hear the blest Supreme
> Lightly appealed to on each trifling theme.
> Maintain your rank, vulgarity despise.
> To swear is neither brave, polite, nor wise."
>
> — COWPER.

QUESTIONS.

What is profanity?
Is it common?
Is it right or wrong?
Do we easily fall into evil speech?
Do we learn it by example?
Is profane swearing justifiable?
Can it be necessary?

Is the habit acquired when we are young?

Can God's name be taken in vain in prayer? Or in singing hymns?

Can one swear without speaking the words?

Is this as bad as spoken oaths?

What is the story of General Washington at his dinner-table?

What effect is swearing likely to have on the character?

Is it likely to lead to other vices?

Is a profane boy a fit companion for others in school or on the playground?

Do boys think it manly to swear?

CONSCIENCE.

That inward feeling which makes us peaceful and happy when we do right, and which condemns us when we do wrong, is conscience.

CONSCIENCE is very faithful; it tells us what we ought to do and what we ought not to do. There are several ways in which conscience is faithful to us.

1. Conscience warns us, before we begin to do wrong. Do you know what warning means? If a man were to see a little girl going towards a deep well, with nothing around it to keep her from falling in, and should tell her to take care and not go there, — that would be warning her. So conscience warns us. When we are about to do anything wrong, — yes, when we are just beginning to think of doing wrong, — conscience warns us not to do it.

A boy was playing in the yard, and he found by the side of the fence a large red apple. He put it in his pocket. He knew that it belonged to another boy; but he thought he would carry it away alone, and eat it after school. Just then the bell rang. He went in and took his seat, with the apple in his pocket.

All that afternoon he was restless and uneasy. There was something in his heart which seemed to say, "That apple is not yours; you must not keep it. You must not eat it after school." This was conscience warning him not to do wrong. For he had not yet actually done anything outwardly wrong. The apple was safe in his pocket. He had not yet had an opportunity to give it to the boy to whom it belonged. He had not yet begun to carry it away to a secret place to eat it. But conscience looked forward to, and warned him against the dishonest act which he was going to do. He tried to amuse himself by thinking of something else; but conscience would not let him rest; until, just before school was over, he resolved that he would carry the apple to the boy who owned it. Then his mind was relieved, and he became quiet in spirit and happy again.

2. Conscience remonstrates while we are doing wrong. Do you know what remonstrates means? Some children walking in a garden, go to a tree and get some apples which are not ripe, and which their father has forbidden them to take. One of the children, more obedient than the rest, says, "You must not take those apples; it is wrong; you ought not to disobey father." This is remonstrating. So conscience remonstrates when we are doing anything wrong. We feel uneasy and unhappy while we are doing it; and we cannot help thinking that it is wrong, and that we ought not to do it.

3. Conscience reproaches us after we have done wrong, and makes us anxious, unhappy and afraid. We are afraid that somebody saw us, or will find out the wrong we have done. We are unhappy. We cannot help thinking of the sin, though we try to forget it. When we are alone, conscience reproaches us; it reminds us of our guilt, and we feel ashamed and wretched. We are afraid. We dare not be alone. We know that we have done wrong, and our hearts sink with fear.

How much better it would be for us always to do right, than thus to wound the conscience, and load our hearts with anxiety and suffering.

4. Conscience becomes quiet again when we confess the wrong that we have done, and resolve to do so no more. Probably the principal reason why conscience is given us, is to prevent our doing wrong; and so, when we cease to do wrong, it ceases to give us pain.

When a boy is only intending to do something wrong, but has not yet begun to do it, and his conscience is warning him, and making him feel restless and uneasy, he can very easily quiet its warnings, and obtain peace of mind again, by giving up his thought of doing wrong, and determining to do right. When he has already done wrong, and injured any one by it, — if he will determine to do so no more, and confess his fault, and make reparation for the injury — then he will be happy again.

A boy found a piece of money in his mother's bureau drawer. He took it and determined to keep it himself. He thought if his father should ask him where he got it, he could tell him that he found it. "For," he said to himself, "I did find it in the drawer." His father did ask him, when he saw him playing with the money; and he told him that he had found it. He felt guilty when he took the money. He felt still more guilty when he told his father that he had found it. Then his father asked him where he found it. He had not expected this question. He was confounded. He answered suddenly, "In the street." His father wondered who could have lost it, but said no more, and so the boy escaped detection.

But though he was pleased that he was not detected, his sense of guilt made him miserable. Every time he felt the money in his pocket, the touch seemed to arouse his conscience to reproach him.

If he had gone at once and returned the money to his father, and confessed that he did not find it in the street, but that he took it from his mother's drawer, he might have been happy again. Instead of that he went and bought nuts with it. Some of the nuts he ate, and the rest he gave to other boys. Thus he fixed the feelings of guilt and wretchedness in his mind; he made conscience his enemy, and prepared himself to commit greater crimes.

A boy once suffered for many months from the reproaches of conscience; and he at last quieted her voice and regained his peace of mind by confessing his sin and making reparation. The case was this : one night he climbed over into a gentleman's garden, not far from the village where he lived, to get some plums. He got his cap full of sweet plums, and came back safely. Conscience warned him not to go; conscience remonstrated with him while he was going, and while he was upon the tree; and conscience bitterly reproached him after the deed was done. The poor boy found that for the sake of a few plums he had almost entirely destroyed his peace of mind. He often thought of his sin at night and when he was alone. He was always afraid when he met the gentleman to whom the garden belonged; and the lane where before he always liked to walk and play, now made him feel so wretched, that he kept away from it entirely.

At last, one day, he went to the gentleman and told

him what he had done. He said he had no money to pay for the plums, but if the gentleman would let him work for him or do errands to make reparation, he would be glad to do it.

The gentleman said that he was very glad that the boy had come and confessed his fault; that he would willingly forgive him; and that he need not come and work for him, for he did not wish him to make any reparation. But the boy replied that he wanted very much to pay him for the plums, and that if the gentleman had any work for him to do, he wished he would let him do it. So the gentleman let him work for him two hours one afternoon. By this means the boy's peace of mind was restored; and he loved to play in the green lane as well as ever.

Thus conscience utters warnings and remonstrances, to prevent us from doing wrong. And if we will cease to do wrong and be faithful in doing our duty, she will restore our peace of mind, and cheer and encourage us by her approval. Peace of mind and a quiet conscience are of inestimable value. Without these, all other means of enjoyment will fail of making us happy; and with them, whatever other privation we may suffer, life will pass pleasantly.

QUESTIONS.

What is conscience?
What is warning?
What does conscience do when we think of doing wrong?
What is the story of the boy and the apple?
What should we do when we find anything?
What does conscience do while we are doing wrong?

What does conscience do after the wrong is done?
What brings peace of mind?
What is the story of the piece of money?
What did the boy gain?
What did the boy lose?
What is making reparation?
What is the story of the plums?
What did that boy gain?
What did he lose?
What does this story illustrate?
Is peace of mind desirable?

CONSCIENTIOUSNESS.

Conscientiousness is obeying conscience. It is being strict and faithful in doing what is right, with a determination not to do what is wrong, — conscience being the judge.

OUR last lesson explained, in general, the nature and powers of conscience. One who is conscientious will obey this voice strictly in regard to all his duties. Whenever he has a secret feeling that anything which he is tempted to do is wrong, he will not do it; and on the other hand, whatever he inwardly feels to be his duty, that he will at all times faithfully perform.

A fixed and steady principle of conscientiousness, with the Divine help, is the only safe guide; for it is plain that any rules of conduct which can be given must be very general. As to almost all the particular acts which we perform, their being right or wrong depends upon the circumstances of each case, and upon the secret intention. A boy on his way to school is standing still, in the street. Is he doing right or wrong? If you say he is doing wrong, it may be answered, perhaps not; he may be waiting for his little brother who is behind, having ample time yet to get to school in season. Do you say he is doing right! Perhaps not. It may be that he is idling away his time, watching a monkey on a hand-organ; or looking to see if some other boys are coming, that he may stop and play with them upon the way; and he may be late at school. Thus the guilt or the innocence of the act depends upon the intention of his mind.

Two boys in the winter, come to a pond. One road leads around the pond, and the other goes across, upon the ice. Neither of the boys has received any directions from his father which way to go. One supposes his father would prefer him to go around the pond, notwithstanding the distance, rather than venture upon the ice. The other supposes that his father considers the ice perfectly safe, and would wish to have him go across it to save time. If the two boys go down to the shore, and one after the other goes upon the ice, we should see no difference between them. One acts just like the other. All that we see in both cases is the same; but the act, though apparently the same in each, would be right in the case of one boy, and wrong in the other.

Thus it is with most of our actions. Whether they are right or wrong cannot be decided by their outward appearance. It depends upon circumstances seen and unseen, and upon the hidden intent and purpose of the mind. Rules, therefore, cannot be given to govern every case. Conscience, or the inward sense of right and wrong, will decide. This power of our minds will be ready to act in each particular instance, and will vary its directions according to the nature of the case. It will tell one boy, who is standing still, on his way to school waiting for his little brother, that he is right. It will tell the other, who is standing the next day in the same place, and in the same attitude, that he is wrong.

When the two boys come down to the shore, conscience will discriminate between the cases, and say to one that if he wishes to be dutiful and obedient as a son, he must not go around the pond, — he must go across ; and to the other, that if he would be dutiful and obedient, he must not go across, but around. Whoever desires to obey this inward monitor, — and wishes, wherever there is a right and a wrong, to do the right, and to avoid the wrong, — is conscientious. He is governed by his sense of duty.

Conscientiousness is a right principle of action, and it ought to be the strongest. There are, however, many other principles. In other words, if we do anything because we ought to do it, or if we do not do it because we ought not to do it, we are conscientious ; but there may be many other motives for doing or not doing things. And many of them are right motives. It is not wrong to be influenced by them; but then we must not mistake them for conscientiousness, and flatter ourselves that we are acting from a sense of duty when we are not. A boy may study diligently in school in order to get a prize, or to rise in the class. This is not wrong; but it is very different from being led to study by a sense of duty. A boy may be very industrious in gathering apples in an orchard for several days, because his father has promised him one bushel for every ten he gathers. It is all very well for him to be influenced by such a motive, but yet the motive is not a sense of duty, — it is hope of reward. There are many other motives which very properly influence us, but they are not sense of duty. A sense of duty may indeed mingle with them, and often does. The boy in gathering his apples may be diligent and faithful, partly because he knows he ought to be, and partly as a means of obtaining the pay. Most good boys would be faithful under the influence of such a double motive, in such a case. And generally, the various motives unite and mingle their influences, in governing our conduct ; and it sometimes requires much skill and pains to separate them, when we are studying our own characters, or investigating the motives of our conduct.

There is one motive that young people very often mistake for conscientiousness, and that is, the wish to be approved by their parents and teachers. This is a good motive. It is right for a child to wish to enjoy the approbation and praise of his father and mother. Suppose they give him, on some afternoon in the spring, the work of putting the yard in order, and raking it over smoothly. He works industriously for several hours, thinking how pleased his parents will be to see how neatly he has done his task. It is the hope of his parents' approval which animates him. True, he does what is right, but he does not do it simply because it is right, but because he loves to see his father and mother pleased. Now, this is a very good motive, — only it is of a different kind from conscientiousness.

But, now, if he should put the yard in order as faithfully and carefully, at some time when his father and mother were away upon a journey, and when there was nobody at home to take any interest in his work, and when his motive for doing so would be simply because it was his duty to do it, and without any hope of reward or praise, — this would be acting from conscientiousness, or a sense of duty. This is a higher motive than the other. It is more noble. He who is under the habitual control of it has an inward principle of moral energy, which carries him onward, whether he is noticed and praised or not. He may like to be noticed and praised, by his parents and teachers. It is very right that he should value their good opinion. But he goes on doing his duty the same, when he expects, and when he does not expect it. And thus, when he leaves home, and goes among people, who would perhaps praise him for doing wrong, he is not led astray by it. His controlling principle is a determination to do what is right.

Thus conscientiousness is a very elevated and noble principle of action. But it may be diseased and so lead a person astray. A boy may be so anxious and afraid lest he should do wrong in some cases, as to be prevented from doing right. Persons sometimes carry their scrupulousness so far, as to make it a source of unnecessary inconvenience and trouble to themselves and their friends. There are several ways in which such a spirit may show itself.

Sometimes persons have a morbid or diseased conscientiousness, in respect to truth. They are afraid to say that a thing is, or that it is not, because they are not absolutely certain. A man, away from home, is asked if his family is well. He is afraid to say "Yes," because he is not sure that something may not have happened since he left home, half an hour before, —and so he would be very careful to say that he believed they were well, or that they were well when he left home. There are many such cases, where we say that a thing is true, when we have evidence that it is true, even although it is barely possible that it may be otherwise. Thus, a boy carrying his dinner along to school tells another boy that he is going to stay at noon ; or says that his sister, who is coming behind him, has two apples in her basket ; — or, a man who has made all his arrangements for taking a journey to the city the next day, says to his neighbors, that he shall certainly go, whatever the weather may be ; or he might say, that he should probably be back in a week, and certainly in a fortnight. Or, if he were standing by a fording-place in a river, where he had often crossed, and a traveller should come down and inquire, he might say that it was perfectly safe. In all these cases, it is right to assert positively ; and yet strictly speaking, the certainty is not absolute. In the last case, for instance, it is barely possible that the current, or some other cause, may have so altered the bed of the river, since the man crossed, as to make it not perfectly safe now. Still, the probability of this is so faint, that it is not to be regarded. The doubt is so small that we cannot express it, without expressing too much. If we say, in such a case, that we suppose the ford is safe, or we have very little doubt that it is safe, we make the traveller think there is some appreciable danger. So we convey a wrong meaning by being too anxious to convey exactly the right one. We must therefore use language in all such cases just as other persons use it, and they will understand us. When we say, in ordinary conversation, that a thing is so, or that it is not so, all that we mean, and all that other persons understand us to mean, is, that we have satisfactory reasons for believing that it is as we say. Extraordinary possibilities are not taken into account. Conscientiousness in regard to all duties, ought to be enlightened and reasonable. We must not be excessively scrupulous about trifling things and little points of form ; but our sense of duty must rest on solid grounds, and we must act in reference to what is essential in principle and substantial in fact.

QUESTIONS.

What is conscientiousness?

Can rules be given for all our conduct?

Does the character of an act always depend upon the outward appearance of it?

How is this shown by the boy on his way to school?

What principle does this case illustrate?

What is the only right principle of action?

Name some of the other principles of action.

What motive may be mistaken for conscientiousness?

How is this shown by the boy working in the yard?

May conscientiousness be diseased?

Name some instances of this.

DUTY TO PARENTS.

Children are dependent on their parents for food, clothing, and instruction. They should, therefore, submit to their authority, and love and honor them.

1. Children ought to submit to parental authority. To submit is to yield a willing and cheerful obedience. The child who openly disobeys his father or mother is guilty of great sin. He is not submissive. He rebels against the authority of his parents, and thus breaks the command of God. So with the child who secretly disobeys. If we obey our parents while in their presence, and disobey when we are not observed, we fail in our duty. It is wrong to disobey, openly or secretly, those who are placed over us with the right to command.

Children often show a want of submission to the authority of their parents, when they do not actually disobey them, either openly or in secret. For, true submission will lead them, not only to obey commands, but to do it cheerfully and pleasantly. If a child, when her mother calls her in from play, comes in with a discontented and ill-natured look, she is not submissive. She is not openly disobedient, but her heart rebels. It is wrong to allow even the heart to rebel against a father or mother.

It is absolutely necessary that children should not only be clothed, fed, sheltered, and instructed in duty,

but that they should be governed.   We see this necessity very early.   Just so soon as the young child begins
to act at all, it is necessary that he should be controlled.
He is creeping upon the floor, perhaps, scrambling along
as fast as he can go towards the fire.   Now, will it do
to argue with him ?   Will it do to instruct him ?   Will
it do to persuade him ?   No ; nothing will do but to
control him.   He must be stopped by authority, if he
has been taught to submit to authority ; and, if not, by
force.   His mother must say sternly, " No, no, — you
must not go there."   He cannot understand the words ;
but he may understand the look and tone and manner,
and may voluntarily submit to authority.   If not, he
must be turned away from danger by force.

When children grow older, there is no longer any
need of parental authority to keep them from going
into the fire.   That danger they have learned to understand and avoid.   But there are other dangers which
they are apt to run into.   A boy of ten years of age
wants to be out in the streets in the evenings to play
with other boys.   If he is allowed to do it, unless he is
in good company, it will be very likely to corrupt and
ruin him.   He cannot see the danger.   It is concealed
from his view.   He cannot be convinced that it is un-
safe ; he cannot be persuaded to give up his wish to be
out at night without leave.   He must be controlled.
His parents must have authority, not arguments, to
depend upon ; or else he will burn himself with a fire
far worse than that in the stove.

There are many difficulties and dangers that children
are exposed to, which they cannot see or understand.
And in the same manner, they cannot see the necessity

or value of the instruction which it is necessary for them to receive. When they are learning the alphabet, how little idea can they form of the pleasures and advantages of being able to read! It is the same with all the studies of later years. Children cannot realize the value of knowledge sufficiently to induce them, of their own accord, to make the necessary effort to obtain it.

If young people were allowed to do as they please about attending to their studies, how soon would spelling-books and slates be laid aside, and the schoolrooms deserted! It is not reasonable to expect in children, the foresight and the consideration and the firmness of purpose necessary to induce them, of their own accord, to make the effort, and submit to the self-denial, necessary to acquire knowledge and to form virtuous habits. Very few children will take medicine when they are sick, unless they have been trained to obedience. It is absolutely necessary, therefore, that children should be controlled by parental authority. They ought to see and acknowledge the necessity, and always submit readily and cheerfully.

2. Children should respect and honor their father and mother. It is very wrong ever to speak disrespectfully to them. Children often do this, sometimes when they are displeased, and sometimes from thoughtlessness. But it is always wrong. If they answer their parents in an ill-natured manner, or express feelings of dislike or resentment, or make them subjects of jest or ridicule, or trifle with their feelings in any way, they do wrong. Such treatment is entirely inconsistent with the principles which ought to govern the intercourse between the child and its parent.

It is wrong, also, to be disrespectful towards parents in speaking of them to others. If a child, whose mother had told him to do something which he did not like to do, were to control his displeasure while in her presence, and then go into another room, or out of doors, and use disrespectful or contemptuous expressions in speaking of her, he would do very wrong. He would break God's command, which requires him to honor his father and mother.

Children should treat their parents with respect as well in their manner towards them, as in their words; that is, be silent when they are speaking; come at once when they call; bring them a seat when they are standing; not come in their way when they are busy; nor interrupt them when they are reading; nor be eager to argue with them, nor contradict anything they say. By observing these principles and treating parents with respectful attention, children can give them great pleasure. For nothing gives parents higher enjoyment than to be honored by their children.

3. Children ought to give very ready and careful attention to their parents' instructions. They are very dependent for all they learn, upon the instruction which their parents give them, and they ought to receive these instructions with docility and readiness. And yet, sometimes children do not wish to learn what their parents teach them. Sometimes they think there is a better way than that which they recommend; so they do not follow their directions. There was a boy who was left-handed. He had had great inconvenience and trouble from it. When he was very young, his mother told him that it would be better for him to learn to use his right hand. She tried to persuade him to change

the habit which he was gradually forming of giving his
left hand the preference; but he would not make any
effort.   He thought his mother was mistaken.   He
could not see why it was not as well to use one hand
as another; and so he went on, making no effort to
change, until, at length, he became incurably left-handed.
When he grew up and experienced the inconvenience
and awkwardness of his habit, he was very sorry that
he had been so foolish when he was young, as to think
that he knew better than his mother.   His repentance
came too late.

Whatever a good father or mother recommends, be
sure to do.   Whatever the way may be in which they
direct you to do anything, do it in that way.   Whenever
they give you any information or advice, listen to it
attentively, treasure up the information in the mind,
and follow the advice faithfully.   This is the only course
that is wise and safe, and what is more important still,
it is the only one that is right.

4. Children ought to be grateful to their parents for
all their kindness and care.   It is true that it is the duty
of parents to provide for their children; but in doing
it they do not act coldly and formally, as if they were
merely discharging a duty; their hearts are filled with
warm affection and love.   How tenderly will a mother
watch over her sick child in its cradle!   She sits by its
side, gently soothing its uneasiness and pain while it is
awake, and watching it while it sleeps.   She hushes
every noise, keeps off every breath of cold air, bathes
the little sufferer's face and hands to soothe its restless-
ness, carries it back and forth across the room with its
cheek upon her shoulder until her arms ache with the

fatigue, and at midnight when she lies down to rest, the least movement at its cradle brings her to its side.

When this child has recovered from his sickness and has grown to be a large boy, and his mother is sick in her turn, will he, instead of being a comfort and a blessing, make himself a source of trouble and care? Will he disturb her quiet by his loud voice and noisy plays, and add to the troubles of the family by his unreasonable requests, his complaints, his fretfulness, and his insubordination? No; not if he is grateful. He will remember his mother's kindness and love to him, and will rejoice in the opportunity to make a kind return. He will be quiet and still. He will move gently from room to room, trying to be useful, and to do something to express his affectionate interest in her, who has been so devoted in her attachment to him. And he will succeed. His conduct will revive and cheer his mother's heart.

When we think how much fatigue and anxiety and suffering, parents endure for their children, it would seem at first, that they never can be repaid; yet when we consider how much power children have to gladden their parents' hearts and lighten their labors and cares, by kind and affectionate and dutiful behavior, we are almost ready to believe that they may fully compensate them day by day. Children do not know how much pain they give their parents by unkindness, ingratitude, and neglect; nor can they realize how great a source of enjoyment they become, when they are docile, obedient, dutiful, and grateful for the kindnesses they receive.

QUESTIONS.

What is the first duty of children toward their parents?

What is it to be submissive?

Is there more than one way of being unsubmissive?

Must children be governed?

How early is this necessary?

Give an illustration.

When children grow older, must they still be controlled?

Why was it right to prevent the boy from playing in the street in the evening?

Can children be kept from harm by persuasion alone?

Can children understand the dangers to which they are exposed?

Would they always avoid them if they could?

What is meant by respecting and honoring parents?

In what ways may children show disrespect?

How should children receive their parents' instructions?

What reasons have children for feeling grateful to their parents?

FORGIVENESS.

When a person has suffered an injury from another, and considers and treats the offender as if he had not done the wrong, — this is forgiveness.

THERE are three courses that we can take as to the injuries done to us by others. We can forgive them freely ; we can punish them and also forgive ; we can take revenge.

1. When we forgive an injury, we no longer feel any anger or ill will toward the person who has done it. We consider how often we ourselves have done wrong, and so we forgive him who has injured us, and dismiss from our minds all thought of doing him any injury.

2. When we deliberately and honestly think that the evil which any person has done, will be likely to be done again by himself, or that the example will be imitated by others, unless the guilty one suffers some penalty ; and when we have a right, by our being the parent, or guardian, or teacher of the one who has done wrong, to inflict the penalty ; and when we do it honestly, for the sake of doing him or others good, and not to gratify our bad passions, then we do right to punish. Pain inflicted, not angrily as a retaliation, but calmly and deliberately as a remedy, is punishment. Some persons have a right to punish, and some have not. Parents and guardians have a right by nature and by the law of God

to punish their children, and masters have the right by law to punish their apprentices. Teachers have it by delegation, — that is, parents and guardians, by sending the children to school, delegate or commit the right to punish them to the teacher. In all cases punishment should be followed by full forgiveness, as soon as the offender expresses his sorrow and repentance.

3. Revenge is very different from punishment. It is inflicting pain upon those who have injured us, not to do them good, nor to prevent others from following their example, but to requite them for the harm they have done us. Thus there is a great difference between revenge and punishment. Punishment tends to make the subject of it better; revenge tends to make him worse. Punishment, if it is actual punishment, and is inflicted with feelings of compassion, does not irritate and enrage the one who suffers it, but it subdues and softens him. If it is not inflicted with calmness and compassion, there is revenge mixed with it, and that prevents the proper effect. For revenge, whether alone or connected with punishment, tends to stir up the bad passions of the one who suffers. It arouses him to anger or else to secret hatred and ill will; and so it perpetuates evil passions and bitter strife.

If, after a person has done us an injury, we go from one to another of our acquaintances, complaining of it in harsh and angry language and endeavoring to make others dislike him, it is revenge. Anything whatever that is intended to give pain, and which expresses our anger and ill will, is of the nature of revenge. And in whatever form it appears, its influence is evil. It does not tend to soften or mitigate the evil, but to

aggravate, to extend, to perpetuate it. Revenge puts
oil upon the flames of discord ; punishment sometimes
puts on water; but forgiveness causes them to die away
of themselves.

In almost all cases where one does wrong, there are
some circumstances which extenuate the guilt, — that is,
which lessen it ; and there are other circumstances which
aggravate the guilt, — that is, they magnify it, make it
appear greater than it really is.   A boy, one afternoon,
when his father was sick, instead of going to school,
went away to play, persuading his younger brother to
go with him.   In the middle of the afternoon he began
to be sorry for his fault ; and though he did not dare to
go into school then, he came home and went to work in
the garden, telling his brother that he was sorry that
he had persuaded him not to go to school, and that he
was determined never to do so again.   In such a case
it would be right to consider some of the circumstances
as aggravating, and some as extenuating the offence.
His father's sickness is an aggravating circumstance ;
it makes the guilt greater.   For it is more criminal to
take advantage of a time of sickness and suffering in
the family, to commit so wrong an act, than it would
be to do the same thing at any ordinary time.   It was
an aggravation of the offence also, for the boy to lead
his younger brother astray with him.   On the other
hand, his coming back early and going to work in the
garden and expressing his sorrow for his fault to his
brother, and promising to do so no more, are extenuating
circumstances.   They make his guilt less than it would
have been if he had persisted in his sin to the last.

If we wish to form a just judgment of any wrong

act, we must become acquainted with, and consider all the circumstances of the case, — those that extenuate and those that aggravate the offence. If we are ignorant of the extenuating circumstances, we shall think the person more criminal than he is. If we are ignorant of the aggravating circumstances, we shall think him less criminal than he is. But the fact is, we seldom do examine the case fully. In the offences which we commit against others, we remember and explain to our friends all the extenuating circumstances, and pass over and forget those which aggravate the guilt. But in the faults which others commit against us, our minds dwell on the aggravations, and we complain of them bitterly to others, while we take no notice of the circumstances which extenuate the fault. And, in regard to the wrongs which we hear of by report, we are often satisfied to take the story just as it comes, with only a very few of the circumstances related to us; and so we form our judgment hastily from a very imperfect knowledge of the facts. One person hears the circumstances which tend to diminish the guilt, and another, those that increase it; and each forms a decided opinion, from the imperfect account which he himself has heard.

Now it will help us very much to exercise a mild and forgiving spirit towards those who have injured us, if we take pains to ascertain and consider calmly, all the extenuating circumstances of the case, and make all the excuse for them that we possibly can. If they acted in any way under a mistake, if we gave them any provocation, if they had been badly brought up, so as not to have had good opportunities to learn how they ought to act towards others, or whatever may have been the extenuating circumstances, we must take pains to think of them all, and to allow them their full weight. This will moderate our displeasure and make it easier for us to forgive.

The grandest example of forgiveness ever known was that of Jesus Christ praying for the forgiveness of his executioners. And it is noticeable that he spoke not of the circumstances which aggravated their guilt, but of those which might in some slight degree excuse it. "Father, forgive them," said he, "for they know not what they do." Their ignorance of the tremendous consequences of the deed which they were committing was a slight extenuation of it.

We ought to follow this example. We must make many excuses in our minds for others, and few for ourselves. When we are injured, we must seek for considerations to diminish the guilt of those who injure us. We must make all the allowances for them that we can. What we cannot excuse, we must forgive ; and we must pray that God will forgive the offenders.

QUESTIONS.

What are the three courses which we can take, in respect to those that do wrong?

What is it to forgive an injury?

What is it to punish an injury?

Have all persons a right to punish?

What persons have a natural right to punish?

What is meant by delegation?

What persons have a delegated right to punish?

Have children ever any right to punish?

What case is mentioned as an illustration of this?

What is revenge?

When punishment is inflicted with feelings of irritation and anger, what is said of it?

What different modes of revenge are mentioned?

What is meant by extenuating circumstances?

What is meant by aggravating circumstances?

Why ought we to take both into the account in judging of an action?

Describe the case of the truant boy.

What were the extenuating circumstances?

What were the aggravating circumstances?

Which do we, generally, take most into the account, in our own case?

Which in the case of other persons who do us injury?

What ought we to do in such cases?

What is said of Jesus Christ's forgiveness?

GRATITUDE.

When we receive a gift or benefit from another, we ought to show kindness and good feeling in return. This is gratitude.

GRATITUDE is one of the highest virtues, pleasant to feel, pleasant to show, pleasant to realize ; while its opposite, ingratitude, is vile, base, dark, and hideous.

Gratitude must be developed by careful training. There are many ways by which children can show gratitude to their parents ; such as good behavior, industry, good service, and others. The love which a very young child feels towards its mother from the beginning has nothing like gratitude in it. After a time when the child learns to think, it can be told how much its mother has done for it, and then, if properly instructed, it will begin to see what gratitude is. And this is so with many who are no longer young. They receive many gifts and benefits with no thought of doing any kindness in return. We need not go far to find instances of this. We often receive kindness, and think the debt is paid by the expression of thanks, and take no pains to show kindness in return. A teacher is at great pains to make a lesson plain to a boy, but the boy does not always say even as much as " Thank you." Nor is the pupil more careful after this, to behave better or study more diligently. Gratitude is not only what we feel in return for what we receive from others, but it is a desire to do something in return, to show that we have this feeling.

A young boy, who has been nursed through a long and severe illness by a sister older than himself, will no doubt often say that he is grateful for her kindness ; but if he is not more careful ever after, to please her and help her as much as he can, it cannot be said that he is grateful. Nothing that he can do is too much, in return for the great care and nursing she gave him, while he was so sick and helpless.

A boy who is poor and without friends to give him a start in work or business, finds employment with a merchant who treats him kindly and gives him opportunities for advancement. He works faithfully for his employer, and is successful in reaching a higher place in the store. He knows that he is indebted to his friend for his success, and he says so, more than once, while everything goes on well. After a time the merchant fails in business, and after trying to recover himself, sinks in despondency and dies, leaving his family in poverty. The young man goes elsewhere, is quite successful, and becomes very prosperous. One day a son of his former master calls upon him for employment, and he tells him that he has no vacancy in his store, and he can do nothing for him. If he had been truly grateful, he would have used all the means in his reach to help the son of his benefactor. Here was no gratitude for the kindness shown to him when he was poor and friendless.

Ingratitude is very common. Young people often forget the kindness, the love, the care, of their parents. All these seem to come as a matter of course, for they come every day, and it is easy to forget from whom they come. A boy was bathing in a stream, and getting into deep water, and not being able to swim, was just about to sink and be drowned, when his teacher plunged in and saved him. For many days after this, the boy felt very grateful to his teacher and gave him no trouble in the school ; but he was usually an idle, lazy boy, and after a while he forgot how much he owed his teacher, and fell back into his old indolent habits.

A gentleman who is interested in boys helps one to get a good situation. The boy has few friends who are able to help him, and he accepts the place procured for him with great pleasure. There are many reasons why he should do his very best in all things, to please his. employer and succeed in the business, whatever it is ; and one especially is, that by faithful labor and care, he can show his gratitude to his friend who got the place for him ; but after a while he becomes so care- less and idle that he loses his place, and when his friend reasons with him and reproves him for his folly, he treats him with indifference and will not take his advice.

One cold night a man who had lost his way in the woods, saw a light in the distance, and going towards it, found a farmhouse. The farmer took him in and gave him a good supper and a place to sleep. In the morning, rising up before the family, the stranger stole the silver spoons which he had seen put in a drawer, and went off.

A watchmaker had a son who was a Sunday-school scholar. One day there came to the Sunday-school a strange boy, who said he had recently come from Eng- land, and that he was poor and friendless. The watch- maker's son took the strange lad home with him, and his father was so much interested in the stranger, that he offered him a place in his store and gave him his meals at his own house. The stranger made himself very useful to his kind friend, and, continuing in the Sunday-school, made many friends there, who gave him books, and in other ways showed their confidence and their interest in him. After some months the watchmaker had such trust in his clerk, that he allowed him to put the valuable goods in the safe before shutting up the store at night. But one evening, while pretending to do this, the young clerk secreted and stole some of the most valuable watches and rings, and disappeared. All these are instances of ingratitude.

The highest kind of gratitude is that which we owe to God. He is our Creator — our constant Benefactor. He continues us in life, He preserves us in health, He gives us sleep when we are tired, He awakens us in the morning. In some respects sleep is like death. We should never awake, if God did not awaken us. He protects us in danger, He feeds us, He clothes us, He gives us the right use of our minds and of all our bodily faculties.

Gratitude is the easiest of all the virtues to cultivate. It requires no self-denial ; it brings its own reward immediately ; it is within the reach of everybody. There is no one who does not receive some favor or kindness from some other person, and there is no one who cannot say, "I thank you." And if these words are sincerely spoken, and if the conduct is what it ought to be, it is what is meant by gratitude.

QUESTIONS.

What is gratitude?
Is ingratitude very common?
Is it partly due to thoughtlessness?
Who saved the boy about to be drowned?
What was the effect upon the boy?
How did the boy treat the friend who found a place for him?
How did the stranger treat the hospitable farmer?
What is the story of the watchmaker's boy?
Who has the highest claim upon our gratitude?   Why?
Is gratitude a difficult virtue to cultivate?
Does it do good to giver and receiver?

PURITY.

Purity is freedom from all such thoughts, words, and actions as modesty and delicacy condemn; it is to avoid these things ourselves and never willingly to witness them in others.

THE sins against purity, which may be committed by the young, cannot be particularly explained to them, because our instinctive sense of modesty and propriety forbids it. But though the boy, as he advances into life, has to encounter dangers against which he cannot be particularly warned by his teachers or parents, God has given conscience special charge to watch him, and to give him plain warning, in every case when he begins to go astray.

As to most of the other faults and sins that young people are in danger of committing, they seem to need instruction and information more than they do about this. An ignorant boy might, possibly, do some dishonest or unjust things, without being aware that they were dishonest or unjust. He needs to have some things particularly explained to him, in order that their true character may be known. But, as to all actions, and words, and thoughts, which are immodest and impure, he knows that they are so by instinct; that is, as the birds know how to build their nests, — by a natural impulse, without ever being taught. His shame, his downcast looks, his careful concealments, all show that he knows perfectly well that he is guilty, though no parent or teacher may have pointed out to him the guilt. Nature points it out to him. Nature, even if the parents do not give him minute instruction, takes effectual care to give it to him herself; and he cannot sin, either in thought, word, or deed, in the most secret manner, without feeling self-condemned and ashamed.

The various kinds of sin which children commit in childhood are only beginnings. They are very bad in themselves, but they lead on to what is very much worse. If a father detects his son in stealing some fruit from the storeroom, the sorrow that he feels is not so much for the loss of the fruit; nor is it, perhaps, altogether on account of the guilt his son has incurred by that one sin. He looks forward. He sees all the successive steps of dishonesty, as they are likely to be developed in future years, and he is overwhelmed with the fear, that his son may grow up to be a thief. He has a distinct idea of the depths of guilt and suffering which such a beginning leads to, and the companions, the haunts, the vices, the shame, the trial, the prison, the punishment, and all the multiplied miseries of such a career. The boy himself, however, cannot understand all this. He may know something of it in general; but he cannot form any distinct and clear ideas, of the extent and variety of the sufferings which he is bringing upon himself, when he begins to be dishonest; that is, he enters upon a course of sin, while he has not, and while it is impossible that he can have, any idea of the awful penalties which God has annexed to it, and which will certainly come upon him if he goes on.

And this is still more strikingly the case in respect to

impurity. It seems to the young to be wrong, but harmless; they cannot shut their eyes to the guilt of it; but they have no reason to suppose that it is likely to be attended with very serious consequences. This seems to be a case where God has made known to them the law very distinctly, but has concealed the penalty. Conscience charges them, in the most solemn manner even at the tenderest age, not to do, not to say, not to think, what the instinctive sense of modesty and propriety forbids; but there is no way by which they can form any clear conception of the terrible sins and miseries, to which such things lead. The child who begins by loving to hear impure language, and then gradually learns to use it himself, commences a course which ends in vices, and crimes, and sufferings, of which he can form no idea. The remorse, the shame, the abandoned company, the bodily suffering, the horrible diseases, the wretchedness and degradation, which a life of impurity brings, would terrify the soul of every guilty boy, if it were possible, at his early age, that he could understand and realize them. The most degraded, and miserable, and wretched men and women that are to be found in the world, are made so by the consequences of impurity.

But young people can only have a very general idea of these consequences. They are not old enough to understand how the use of language which they know is wrong, but which seems to do no immediate injury, will lead them on from sin to sin, until it ends in the very extreme of human degradation and misery. When the end comes upon them, they say, that if they had only known, they would not have commenced so awful a career. If they had only known! But they did know the guilt, though they did not know the penalty. The beginnings may have seemed harmless, it is true ; that is, the first offences appeared not to do any immediate injury. But they never could have seemed innocent. Conscience was always ready to testify that they were very, very wrong. They have, therefore, in their sufferings, no cause to complain of the justice of God. When He clearly makes known His commands, they who dare to disobey them, do it at their own peril. They cannot complain if awful consequences follow, which they could not possibly have foreseen.

Let young people, then, be pure, — pure in thought, pure in word, and pure in deed, — and let them close their ears against all impure words, and their eyes against all impure reading and pictures. Then they. will escape present guilt and shame, and future vice and misery.

There is often conversation of an indelicate nature among boys, conversation which they would be very unwilling that their father or mother should hear : without great care in early life, their minds will be so poisoned and corrupted in this way, that it will be a calamity to them all their lives. They will, during all the years of manhood, have cause to mourn that such impure words and thoughts ever entered the mind. There is hardly anything more important to the welfare and happiness of a boy than a caution on this subject. He cannot be too careful to avoid all such words and thoughts. He should never utter a word of this character which he would not be willing to repeat to his parents. He cannot understand the dreadful consequences of having

an impure mind. It would be far less a calamity to lose
a foot, or a hand, or an eye, than to lose delicacy and
purity of mind. When we think of the temptations
to which boys are exposed in this respect, the bad boys
with corrupt hearts, whom they must inevitably meet,
the indelicate words they must almost unavoidably hear,
we cannot too earnestly warn them of their danger.
When they are present where such conversation is
going on, they should escape if they possibly can.
They should resolve that they will not listen to that
which conscience tells them to be wrong. And conscience will be very faithful on this subject. It warns
loudly and earnestly, whenever the approach is made
to the region of impropriety. If a boy indulges himself
in this sin, he will not do it ignorantly, and he will
suffer for it as long as he lives. Many a good man has
been unable, even to the end of his life, to blot out from
his mind, the impressions left there by impure thoughts.

Dr. Johnson was once in company, where a person
related an anecdote which was of an indelicate character.
As soon as he had finished, Dr. Johnson, sternly looking
at him, said, "Sir, if you ever intend to repeat that
anecdote in my presence, I will thank you to inform me
of it, that I may leave the room. Such thoughts cannot
pass through the mind without leaving a trace of pollu-
tion behind them." And more recently, at a dinner-table,
one of the guests after looking around before he began
to tell an indelicate story, said, "I believe there are no
ladies present." "No," said another guest, "but there
are gentlemen present"; and so he prevented the story.
And any one who has self-respect, be he man or boy,
will spurn the language of impurity.

If any boy should fall into this habit of foolish and wicked talk, and should let it grow upon him, as it surely will, he cannot hope that his teachers or other instructors will respect him ; that any right-minded man will ever want his services, however valuable those services may be, or however useful he might be. And let him remember also, what is of vastly more consequence than anything in this world, that when he comes to stand before God on the judgment day, with such evil habits clinging to him not repented of, he cannot enter into the kingdom of heaven.

QUESTIONS.

What is meant by instinctive?

Does a child know what impurity is without being taught?

How does conscience protect him?

Do children know all the consequences of the sins they commit?

Could they understand them if they were explained?

Is this any excuse for committing the sin?

Ought children to associate with those that use improper language?

Ought they to listen to immodest talk?

What did Dr. Johnson once say on this subject?

What did the guest at dinner say?

REPENTANCE.

All people frequently fall into temptation and do wrong. They ought always to be sorry for it, acknowledge it, and resolve to do so no more.

ALL persons often do wrong. One great difference between the good and the bad, is, that the good acknowledge the wrong, and at once return to their duty ; but the bad persist, and make false excuses, and are angry at being reproved, and continue in their wrong-doing.

When we are reproved for a fault, we should never hastily deny or·begin to excuse what we have done. If there is a misunderstanding of the case, so that we are really innocent, when we are supposed to be guilty, it is certainly right that we should, in a gentle and proper manner, make the truth known. But such cases are rare. The excuses and defences which children generally make, arise merely from their being unwilling to admit that they have done wrong ; they prefer to per-- sist, to disguise or conceal the truth, or to turn the censure off upon some other person.

But it is better to acknowledge the fault. To feel and to express sorrow for wrong-doing is not only the right way to get out of a difficulty, but it is altogether the pleasantest way. It is repentance. Endeavoring to excuse or to hide a fault only prolongs the mental uneasiness which wrong-doing brings. If you are charged with a fault, listen to the charge patiently, consider it candidly, and then, if you see that you have done wrong, fully and freely confess it. You will find that to be the quickest, the easiest, and the pleasantest way of getting out of the difficulty.

It is not enough, however, merely to say that you know you have done wrong. Repentance must be sincere; it must come from the heart. We must feel how evil it is to do wrong, even in what might be considered a trifling matter. A boy pushes his little sister down, because she has done something that he did not like. Now, when he is reproved for it, he ought to think that, though a little push is very trifling, yet that an angry spirit, leading to an act of violence, is very serious. It is the thought as well as the deed, which gives the character to an action; and this we should think of, whenever we have done wrong, and acknowledge, not carelessly and indifferently, but with real sorrow for the wrong spirit which the action showed.

When we are doing wrong, and are told of it, we should immediately and good-humoredly stop, and begin to do right. There are many faults which young people fall into, from thoughtlessness or momentary impulse; and then, if they seem willing to be told of them, and immediately change their course, the evil is kept within very narrow limits. But if they persist in them, and seem displeased at being reproved, it makes the wrong far greater; it changes a mere thoughtless fault to a deliberate and wilful sin.

Therefore, make it a rule to abandon at once whatever you are doing that is wrong, as soon as your attention is called to it by your parent or teacher or by any friend.

This is the way a certain boy received reproof, when his father told him that he was making too much noise with his brother, in the parlor: he immediately ceased making a noise, and went at once, pleasantly, and took a book, and sat down by the fire.

His sister, however, could not bear to be told of her faults. At school, when she was sitting in a wrong attitude, if the teacher called her attention to it, she would look displeased, and change her position as little as possible, without seeming absolutely to refuse to obey. When the teacher asked her to read louder or more slowly in the class, she would change her mode of speaking as little as possible, — thus persisting in the fault, instead of abandoning it. How much better it is to yield at once, with good-humored readiness, than to cling to our faults, and regard, with looks of sullen displeasure, those who point them out to us!

True repentance is essential to restore our peace of mind and happiness, when we have committed any great and serious sins. True repentance makes us willing to see and to admit that we have been guilty; it makes us truly sorry that we have thus yielded to temptation and done wrong, and it makes us desirous to abandon the sinful course at once, and to return to duty. Thus true repentance brings with it reformation; and it leads us. not only to avoid sinning again, but to repair as far as we can whatever injury our sin has already done.

There is a false repentance. That is, there are certain feelings which seem like repentance in some degree, but which really are not, but are something very different. A boy took the key of his own chest, one afternoon, when his father was gone away, and tried to unlock his father's desk with it, to steal some money. He put his key into the lock, but it did not fit exactly, and at length, in turning it, it was caught so that he could not get it either back or forward, and, at last, after trying a long time to get it out, he had to go away and leave it, — his mind in a state of great agitation and terror. He was afraid that his father would come home at night, and find his key in the lock of the desk, and so he would be detected. He was very sorry, indeed, that he had ever attempted such an act. But his feeling was not repentance ; it was fear of detection. He was not troubled by the thought of the wickedness of stealing his father's money, but of the danger that he should be detected and punished. It was remorse and terror, not repentance ; and it did not lead him to confess and forsake his sin, but only to think of every possible way that he could contrive to conceal it.

True repentance is not fear of being detected, nor fear of being punished ; nor is it merely the feeling of guilt and self-condemnation at having done what is wrong. It is such a sorrow for the wrong as leads us to acknowledge, and not to conceal it, and to repair the injury it has done ; and it makes us sincerely desire, and firmly determine, to do so no more.

QUESTIONS.

Do all persons sometimes do wrong?

What is one great difference between the good and the bad, in regard to any wrong which they have done?

What is our duty when we are reproved for our faults?

Which is the right course when we have done wrong, — to acknowledge the fault, or to defend ourselves and make excuses?

Which is the more pleasant course?

State the case of the boy who was told to be quiet.

How did his sister bear reproof?

Can our peace of mind be restored, after we have done wrong, except by true repentance?

What is false repentance?

Describe the case of the boy and the false key.

Was his anxiety, when he found he could not get the key out, true repentance?

What feeling was it?

What does true repentance lead us to do?

DUTY TO GOD.

God is our creator, and we ought to adore Him. He has made laws, and we ought to obey them. He forgives the penitent — He loves all His creatures; and we ought to love Him. He is always near us, and ready to listen to us, and we ought to pray to Him for help, guidance and protection.

No one is able to conceive of the greatness and majesty of God. We cannot understand Him. He has no form or shape like a man. He is everywhere, and knows everything; but He does not see with eyes, or hear with ears, as we do. He is everywhere at the same time. He does not walk from place to place with feet, as we do. His works are going on, too, constantly, in all parts of the universe; but He does not work with hands, as we do. He has no eyes, or ears, or feet, or hands. He has no shape or body. He is a spirit. This is mysterious. It is most difficult to conceive of God.

God is everywhere. You plant a seed in the ground in the spring; there comes from it in a few days a little sprout. There are two parts: the part that is for the root turns down and grows into the ground; the part that is for the stem and leaves turns up, and comes out into the air. How do the root and the stem know which way they must grow? They do not know. God is there, where you plant that seed, and He guides the growing of it; and all over this vast world you cannot find a place where you can put the smallest seed, but God will be always ready there, to send the little leaf-lets up and the root down.

And so God is watching over and sustaining every star that shines in the sky. The stars are great worlds, — very great indeed, — though they are so many millions of miles from us that they look twinkling and small. They are far, very far, away from us; but God is there, always present with every one.

When you see a little cloud floating in the sky, you may know that God is there to form it. He gathers together the little drops of water — so small that they will float, high in the air. He increases the number of them, till the cloud which they form becomes large and black, and He brings down, one by one, every drop that falls in rain. He makes the lightning to flash and the thunder to roll.

While God is in the sky, among the stars, and clouds, and storms, He is also present in every part of the earth and of the deep sea. If we could go off a thousand miles from the shore, and then go down, down, very deep into the ocean, we should find that God is always there. Millions of plants and animals, which we never see or know, He is continually forming there; and He watches and rules over every one of them, as they spend their lives, clinging to the ragged rocks, or gliding through the green waters.

Did you ever feel your pulse? Do you know what makes the pulse beat? It is the throbbing of the blood as it is driven along through a little channel, into your hand. It is by means of this that your hand is kept alive, and warm, and made to grow. Your blood beats

its way thus into every part of your body; and if it
should cease this motion, you would soon become cold
and stiff, and die. Now, who makes your pulse beat?
Do you do it? Can you make it beat, or stop its beating? No. It is God. His power is always present
with you and around you; and He causes the pulse to
beat, all the time, wherever you are, and whatever you
are doing, — whether you are awake or asleep, at home
or abroad, running or playing, or sitting still. How
strange that God should never for a moment forget, and
leave His work undone! He is great and mighty, and
is always present and always acting everywhere. We
ought to adore Him for His greatness and majesty, love
Him for His goodness, dread His displeasure, and ask
His forgiveness and protection every day.

Every duty which we have to perform, is required of
us by God; so that we cannot neglect any duty whatever, without disobeying Him; which is, as it were, a
double sin. If a boy were to make his younger brother
drag him about upon his little wagon, when they were
at play, he would do wrong; he would be unjust and
oppressive to his little brother. If, moreover, his father
had expressly forbidden his doing so, then, in addition
to the sin against the child, he would be guilty of disobedience to his father. Now, the law of God clearly
forbids all the sins of which we can be guilty against
any one; so that we cannot do any wrong without disobeying Him. If a child is unjust to his playmate, he
disobeys and displeases God. If he attempts to deceive
his parents, he disobeys and displeases God. If he
wastes his time, or is insubordinate and troublesome at
school, he disobeys and displeases God. Every offence

which we can commit, small as well as great, is a trans-
gression of His law; and we cannot be really happy after
we have committed such transgressions, until we obtain
His forgiveness. We ought, therefore, to make it the
great duty and business of our lives to secure and enjoy,
at all times, the favor of Almighty God, our Father
in heaven. We should seek His pardon for our sins, go
to him always in our trouble, look to Him for protection
in danger, for strength in temptation, for comfort in sorrow, and for peace and happiness in duty ; and we should
cultivate such constant habits of intercourse and com-
munion with Him, as shall help us, under all the circumstances of life, to feel that He is our refuge and strength,
and a very present help in time of trouble.

QUESTIONS.

What feeling should be awakened in our minds by the power and
majesty of God? By His decision in punishing sin? By His kindness and mercy to us?

What is meant by being a spirit?

What takes place when a seed is put into the ground?

Does this prove that the power of God is present there?

What is said of God's presence in the heavens? In the sea?

What causes the pulsations we feel in the wrist?

Do we keep up these pulsations by our own power?

What would be the consequence if they should cease?

Are we, then, dependent upon God every moment?

What is meant by double criminality?

How is this illustrated by the case of the boy who should compel
his brother to drag him upon his little wagon?

Does the law of God include every duty?

Then, whenever we do wrong, or neglect any duty, do we not
disobey God?

From what we know of God, what five things should we do?

Adore Him. Obey Him. Fear Him. Love Him. Praise Him.

**For additional copies of this book,
or to request our free resource catalog, contact:**

426 Circle Dr. • P.O. Box 397 • Aledo, TX 76008
(800) 873-2845 • (817) 441-6044
www.wallbuilders.com